© Danann Media Publishing Ltd 2023

First published in the UK by Sona Books, an imprint of Danann Media Publishing Limited

WARNING: For private domestic use only, any unauthorised copying, hiring, lending or public performance of this book is illegal

CAT NO: SON0570
Written by: Adrian Besley
Cover design: Darren Grice
Book design: Paul Southcombe
Editor: Martin Corteel
Proof reader: Finn O'Neill

Picture credits

The publishers would like to thank the following sources for their kind permission to reproduce the pictures in this book.

Alamy
Abaca Press
Action Images
Actionplus
Alfo Co. Ltd
Jonathan Larsen
Diadem
PA Images
TT News Agency

Getty
Boris Streubel
Adam Pretty/ALLSPORT
AFP
Andy Lyons
Ben Radford
Brad Smith/ISI Photos
Christof Stache/AFP
David Madison
Eric Verhoeven/Soccrates
Francois Nel
Gualter Fatia
Guang Niu
Hannah Peters – FIFA
Johannes Eisele/AFP
Jose Breton/NurPhoto
Julio Cesar Aguilar/AFP
Kevin C. Cox
Las Baron – FIFIA
Maja Hitij
Naomi Baker – The FA
Octavio Passos
Tim Sloan/AFP
Timothy A. Clary/AFP
Tommy Cheng/AFP

All other pictures
Adrian Furby
Agencia Brasil
Ailura
Alexchen4836
AliveHuman136
Amerpear
Anders Henrikson
Arild Vågen
Astro8652
BaldBoris
Báo Sài Gòn Giải Phóng
Camw
Carlos Figueroa Rojas
Curt Gibbs
Dianaatflourish
Dontworry
El Loko Foto
Erik Drost
Frank Haug
FutbolFoto
G.Garitan
General116
Granada
Happiraphael
IQRemix
James Boyes
Jamie Smed
JaumeBG
Johnmaxmena
Jordieboase
joshjdss
Ladiezfutbolfemenino
Liondartois
LittleBlinky
Marouane Hamousse
Matt Boulton
Mohammed Ayman Nechchad
Nicktwiggy
Noah Salzman
Pierre-Yves Beaudouin
Rcanizares
Rikard Fröberg
Steffen Prößdorf
Ted Eytan
Theanatron
Thewomensgame
Threecharlie
US Embassy Bogota
Vasyatka1
Wilson Dias/Abr
又黑口壳

Every effort has been made to acknowledge correctly and contact the source and/or copyright holder of each picture and Sona Books apologises for any unintentional errors or omissions, which will be corrected in future editions of the book.

All rights reserved. No Part of this title may be reproduced or transmitted in any material form (including photocopying or storing it in any medium by electronic means and whether or not transiently or incidentally to some other use of this publication) without the written permission of the copyright owner, except in accordance with the provisions of the Copyright, Designs and Patents Act 1988.Applications for the copyright owner's written permission should be addressed to the publisher.

The moral right of Adrian Besley to be identified as the author of this work has been asserted by him in accordance with the Copyright, Designs and Patents Act 1988.

Publisher's Note
FIFA Women's World Rankings as released on 24 March 2023.

Made in EU.
ISBN: 978-1-915343-20-8

THE HISTORY OF THE
WOMEN'S WORLD CUP

GREAT MATCHES • STAR PLAYERS • ICONIC MOMENTS • WWC 2023 PREVIEW

THE HISTORY OF THE WOMEN'S WORLD CUP

CONTENTS

8 INTRODUCTION

10 LEGENDS OF THE WOMEN'S WORLD CUP

16 PREVIEW OF THE WOMEN'S WORLD CUP 2023
- 18 The Venues
- 20 Qualification
- 22 Inter-Confederation Play-offs

23 MEET THE TEAMS

24 Group A
- 26 New Zealand
- 27 Norway
- 28 Philippines
- 29 Switzerland

30 Group B
- 32 Australia
- 33 Republic of Ireland
- 34 Nigeria
- 35 Canada

36 Group C
- 38 Spain
- 39 Costa Rica
- 40 Zambia
- 41 Japan

42 Group D
- 44 England
- 45 Haiti
- 46 Denmark
- 47 China

48 Group E
- 50 United States
- 51 Vietnam
- 52 Netherlands
- 53 Portugal

54 Group F
- 56 France
- 57 Jamaica
- 58 Brazil
- 59 Panama

60 Group G
- 62 Sweden
- 63 South Africa
- 64 Italy
- 65 Argentina

66 Group H
- 68 Germany
- 69 Morocco
- 70 Colombia
- 71 South Korea

72 THE HISTORY OF THE WOMEN'S WORLD CUP
- 74 Women's World Cup China 1991
- 82 Women's World Cup Sweden 1995
- 90 Women's World Cup United States 1999
- 98 Women's World Cup United States 2003
- 106 Women's World Cup China 2007
- 114 Women's World Cup Germany 2011
- 122 Women's World Cup Canada 2015
- 132 Women's World Cup France 2019

CONTENTS

THE HISTORY OF THE WOMEN'S WORLD CUP

INTRODUCTION

The FIFA Women's World Cup 2023 in Australia and New Zealand is the ninth edition of the iconic global tournament. It is the biggest yet, the first to be co-hosted and the first to take place in the Southern Hemisphere. It promises to be the most high profile and most-watched competition in its 32-year history.

Mirroring the growth and increasing professionalism of women's football across the globe, the Women's World Cup, held every four years, has grown from 12 teams in the inaugural 1991 tournament to 16 in 1999 and 24 in 2015. The 2023 tournament features 32 teams with many taking part for the first time.

Each tournament has had a greater profile than the last and has reached increasingly more people across the globe. Over 1.2 billion people around the world watched the Women's World Cup 2019 with the final between the USA and The Netherlands reaching more than 80 million viewers. That was more than double the corresponding figures for the 2015 finals. The record audiences for the Women's EURO 2022 competition suggest 2023 will continue this trend (although time difference to Europe and North America may impact viewer numbers).

Through eight tournaments the Women's World Cup has written its own fascinating history which encompasses the great USA team of the 1990s, the German side that won consecutive titles in the 2000s and the fairy story of Japan's 2011 victory. And, it has created its own legends, among them Germany's Birgit Prinz, Mia Hamm of the USA and Brazil's Marta. These pages tell the story of those World Cups and the players who have lit up the competition.

The book also previews the 2023 World Cup. It details the venues and gives an account of each team – their qualification route, their coach and key players and their chances of success. It promises to be an exciting and competitive tournament with more teams than ever having a chance of lifting the trophy.

The Women's World Cup 2023 will feature the greatest players on the planet, including Australia's Sam Kerr, Spain's Aitana Bonmatí, Norway's Caroline Graham Hansen, Germany's Alexandra Popp, Brazil's Debinha and England's Lucy Bronze with USA's Sophia Smith, England's Lauren Hemp, Germany's Julie Brand and Columbia's Linda Caicedo among the young talents who could shine. The finals will also probably be the last chance to see some of the stars of the game on the world stage with world's leading international goalscorer, Canada's Christine Sinclair; USA's two-time World Cup winners Megan Rapinoe and Alex Morgan and Brazilian greats, Cristiane and Marta all set for their swan-songs.

The history of the Women's World Cup is packed with nail-biting excitement, great teams and players, surprises, heartbreak and glory. As the tournament moves to Australia and New Zealand, the stage is perfectly set for the world's best to create their own history in a World Cup to remember.

INTRODUCTION

The United States team celebrate winning their second consecutive World Cup after defeating Netherlands in the 2019 final.

THE HISTORY OF THE WOMEN'S WORLD CUP

WOMEN'S WORLD CUP LEGENDS

The eight Women's World Cup tournaments to date have produced many extraordinary moments, superb goals and breath-taking saves, and made stars of many players, but true World Cup legends come back time and time again to prove their exceptional quality. This selection is not definitive – Canada's Christine Sinclair, England's Kelly Smith, Germany's Heidi Moh and USA's Kristine Lilly, Carli Lloyd and Christie Pearce, among the greats not featured – but it highlights some of those who have written their names into the history of the competition.

WOMEN'S WORLD CUP LEGENDS

THE HISTORY OF THE WOMEN'S WORLD CUP

Michelle Akers
USA

Women's World Cup finals: 1991 (winner), 1995, 1999 (winner)

Selected for the first ever USA squad in 1985, Akers spent 15 years at the top level. Her ten goals at the 1991 Women's World Cup still stands as a record. Two of them came in the 2-1 defeat of Norway in the final, including the winner in the last minutes, when she intercepted a back pass and rounded the keeper. Due to illness, she became a defensive midfielder where her tenacious playing style and aerial dominance made her an indispensable member of the team which made the 1995 finals and won the 1999 tournament. In 2002, she shared the FIFA Female Player of the Century award.

Sun Wen
China

World Cups: 1991, 1995, 1999, 2003

The leader and inspiration of China's great 1990s team, Sun Wen is arguably the best Asian player ever. She was the complete forward; could dribble through defenders, was a phenomenal passer and packed a powerful shot. She scored 11 World Cup goals in 29 games, helping take China to two quarter-finals, a semi-final and the 1999 final, where they lost to USA in a penalty shoot-out, but she still won the Golden Ball (top player) and Golden Boot (top scorer) at that tournament, and would share the FIFA Female Player of the Century award in 2002.

Mia Hamm
USA

World Cups: 1991 (winner), 1995, 1999 (winner), 2003

Mia Hamm played in four World Cup finals, and was a winner in two and a semi-finalist in the others. She had skill, vision and a superb ability to find a shooting chance, scoring eight goals over the course of the four tournaments. As FIFA Women's World Player of the Year for the first two years of the award in 2001 and 2002, she is a legend of the game. Hamm did more than that, though. As the most well known of the victorious 1999 team, she became the first superstar of women's football and used her fame to promote the World Cup and inspire thousands of girls around the world.

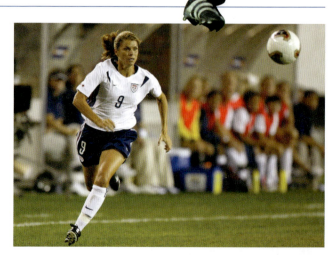

WOMEN'S WORLD CUP LEGENDS

Homare Sawa
Japan
Women's World Cup finals: 1995, 1999, 2003, 2007, 2011 (winner), 2015

Japan's silky and deft forward Homare Sawa was 16 years old when she made her tournament debut in 1995 and 36 when she featured in Japan's defeated final team at her sixth Women's World Cup in 2015. She was a constant star of the team, but it is the 2011 finals for which she will always be remembered. Captaining an unfancied Japan, Sawa scored a group stage hat-trick against Mexico and then inspired the team through to a final against USA, where her audacious flick-volley set up an incredible victory. Sawa was the tournament's top scorer, best player and was named the 2011 FIFA Women's World Player of the Year.

Hege Riise
Norway
Women's World Cup finals: 1991, 1995 (winner), 1999, 2003

An attacking midfielder with an ability to spot a pass and dissect an opposition defence, Riise was the driving force of the great 1990s Norway team. She helped the team reach two finals and one semi-final, her greatest achievement coming in 1995 when she won the Golden Ball and scored five goals from midfield as Norway swept all before them. In their 2-0 final win over Germany, Riise scored one of the best ever World Cup goals, beating three defenders before accurately sliding the ball home from outside the area. She is now head coach of Norway as they hope to rekindle those glory days.

Joy Fawcett
USA
Women's World Cup finals: 1991 (winner), 1995, 1999 (winner), 2003

One of the greatest defenders in the history of women's football, Joy Fawcett was an integral part of the great USA teams of the 1990s. A strong and aggressive centre-back and part of a formidable partnership with Carla Overbeck, she also excelled at right-back in the 1999 finals. After appearing in five of the USA's six games in the 1991 World Cup, including the final, she went on to play every minute of the 1995, 1999 and 2003 finals. She earned 241 caps, retiring from international football in 2004 as the USA's highest scoring defender

THE HISTORY OF THE WOMEN'S WORLD CUP

Abby Wambach
USA

Women's World Cup finals: 2003, 2007, 2011, 2015 (winner)

This USA forward was not known for her silky skills or fancy footwork, but it is difficult to find a more effective striker. Robust, physical, dominant in the air and deadly in front of goal, Wambach scored 14 of her world record 184 international goals (a record now broken by Canada's Christine Sinclair) over four World Cup tournaments. The most memorable strike came in the 2011 Women's World Cup quarter-finals when she bravely rose at the far post to head home an equaliser against Brazil in the dying seconds of extra-time. She was named FIFA Player of the Year in 2012 and finally picked up a winner's medal in 2015.

Birgit Prinz
Germany

Women's World Cup finals: 1995, 1999, 2003 (winner), 2007 (winner), 2011

Strong and fast with a ruthless scoring instinct, Prinz's 14 Women's World Cup goals put her second in the all-time scorers list. She first netted as a 17-year-old and remains the youngest player ever to appear in a Women's World Cup final. In 2003 she was the top scorer and was voted best player as Germany secured their first World Cup triumph. Then, in 2007, as captain she led them back to the final, opening the scoring as they won a successive trophy. Named FIFA World Player of the Year three years running and runner-up another five times, she is an icon of the game.

WOMEN'S WORLD CUP LEGENDS

Nadine Angerer
Germany

Women's World Cup finals: 2003 (winner), 2007 (winner), 2011, 2015

After nearly a decade as Germany's reserve goalkeeper, picking up six major titles, including the 2003 Women's World Cup, in 2007 Angerer finally got her chance to play. She kept a clean sheet in every game Germany played in those finals as they won a successive world title. She was named goalkeeper of the tournament and given the accolade player of the match for the final, where she made a string of sensational saves and denied Marta from the penalty spot. She went on to captain Germany in the 2011 and 2015 finals, and is the only goalkeeper ever to be named FIFA World Player of the Year.

Marta
Brazil

Women's World Cup finals: 2003, 2007, 2011, 2015

Wearing the famous Brazilian number 10 shirt is a massive responsibility, but Marta has succeeded in adding to its iconic status, showing a flair, touch and ingenuity that dazzles defenders and spectators alike. A six-times FIFA Women's World Player of the Year, she has never won a World Cup, but she has lit up the tournament as much as anyone. She won the Golden Ball and Golden Boot in 2007, and scored in five finals with her 17-goal tally a record for women's and men's finals. Now 37, hopefully she can grace one last tournament and perhaps even take home that elusive winner's medal.

THE HISTORY OF THE WOMEN'S WORLD CUP

PREVIEW OF THE WOMEN'S WORLD CUP 2023

Australia and New Zealand welcome 32 teams to the ninth Women's World Cup finals. They include holders USA, Olympic champions Canada, European champions England and eight first-time qualifiers.

PREVIEW OF THE WOMEN'S WORLD CUP 2023

THE HISTORY OF THE WOMEN'S WORLD CUP

THE VENUES

The Women's World Cup 2023 will be played out in stadiums across Australia and New Zealand. While neither of the hosts are renowned football countries, they share a love of sport and are a great destination for overseas visitors. As excitement builds Down Under, advance ticket sales support claims that this will be the 'biggest, best and most successful' edition ever.

The host nations are brought together by the World Cup mascot, a fun, football-loving penguin named 'Tazuni'. Her name is the combination of the 'Tasman Sea', which separates Australia and New Zealand, and 'unity'. Each of the countries will host 16 teams for the group stage; Groups A, C, E and G – including Spain, Japan, USA and Sweden – play in New Zealand, while Groups B, D, F and H – including Canada, England, France and Germany – are based in Australia.

Each of the venues are top class sporting stadiums. Some, such as Stadium Australia or Eden Park are iconic Olympic or rugby union arenas while others have been redeveloped especially for the tournament. FIFA refer to each of them without any sponsored names.

Eden Park
Auckland/Tāmaki Makaurau, New Zealand
Capacity: 48,276
An iconic international rugby union and cricket venue, New Zealand's largest sports stadium will host the opening ceremony and the first 2023 World Cup match and will also be the venue for one of the semi-finals.

Waikato Stadium
Hamilton/Kirikiriroa, New Zealand
Capacity: 25,111
Most famous for hosting rugby union matches including All Blacks internationals, it has also been a venue for the FIFA U-17 Women's World Cup 2008 and the FIFA U-20 Men's World Cup 2015.

Dunedin Stadium
Dunedin/Ōtepoti, New Zealand
Capacity: 28,744

'The Glasshouse' is New Zealand's only covered stadium, it hosted matches in the 2011 Rugby World Cup and in the 2015 FIFA U-20 World Cup.

Wellington Regional Stadium
Wellington/Te Whanganui-a-Tara, New Zealand
Capacity: 39,000

Wellington is the football capital of New Zealand and its imposing bowl stadium is referred to as 'The Ring of Fire' by fans of the men's and women's A-league teams of Wellington Phoenix who call it home.

THE VENUES

Brisbane Stadium
Brisbane/Meaanjin. Australia
Capacity: 52,263

'The Cauldron' is the home of rugby league team Brisbane Broncos. The Matildas have played occasional friendly internationals at the stadium. It is the venue for the third-place-play-off match in the Women's World Cup 2023.

Melbourne Rectangular Stadium
Melbourne/Naarm, Australia
Capacity: 30,052

Rebuilt in 2010 with a unique geodesic design, the stadium is home to top A-League Women's teams Melbourne Victory and Melbourne City and has hosted international football including the opening of the 2015 AFC Asian Cup.

Stadium Australia
Sydney/Gavial, Australia
Capacity: 83,500

The centrepiece of the Sydney 2000 Olympic Games, it has hosted the biggest matches in Australian Football, including a record crowd (36,109) for Australia Women against the USA in November 2021. It will host a semi-final and the final in the Women's World Cup.

Hindmarsh Stadium
Adelaide/Tarntanya, Australia
Capacity: 18,435

The recently redeveloped stadium has been staging football matches since the 1960s. Home to men's A League team Adelaide United, it has also hosted Australia's men's internationals.

Perth Rectangular Stadium
Perth/Boorloo, Australia
Capacity: 22,225

Redeveloped for the finals, this stadium is a long-time top-level football venue. It is home to Perth Glory, whose women's team play major matches here and has hosted Socceroos (Australian men's team) international matches.

Sydney Football Stadium
Sydney/Gavial, Australia
Capacity: 42,512

Rebuilt for the Women's World Cup 2023, the stunning stadium is on the site of a traditional venue for both women's and men's football, including the 2000 Olympic Women's Football Gold Medal match. It will be the venue of Australia's opening game of the tournament.

19

THE HISTORY OF THE WOMEN'S WORLD CUP

QUALIFICATION

World Cup Finals allocation breakdown

2022 AFC Women's Asian Cup
Australia (co-hosts)
China
Japan
Philippines (debut)
South Korea
Vietnam (debut)

2022 Women's Africa Cup of Nations
Morocco (debut)
Nigeria
South Africa
Zambia (debut)

2022 CONCACAF W Championship
Canada
Costa Rica
Haiti (debut)
Jamaica
Panama (debut)
United States

2022 Copa América Femenina
Argentina
Brazil
Colombia

2022 OFC Women's Nations Cup
New Zealand (co-hosts)

2023 FIFA Women's World Cup qualification (UEFA)
Denmark
England
France
Germany
Italy
Netherlands
Norway
Portugal (debut)
Republic of Ireland (debut)
Spain
Sweden
Switzerland

Over 200 nations originally took part in Women's World Cup 2023 qualification through either through UEFA's European qualification tournament or the various continental championships. Although reigning champions USA had to qualify, both co-host nations were guaranteed places.

There were no surprises in the European qualification tournament, as the highest-ranking nation topped each group and earned a finals place. The complicated play-offs for the remaining three places, however, were less predictable. Switzerland, the best team in the play-offs, did take one place; low ranking Republic of Ireland surprised many by taking the other spot, while Portugal were made to take the inter-confederation tournament route. There was no place for Belgium (whose Tessa Wullaert was the tournament's leading scorer), Austria or Iceland who would have hoped to make the finals.

As tournament hosts Mexico were hotly fancied in the CONCACAF competition, but not only failed to qualify, but also missed out on an inter-confederation play-off place. Chile, who played in their first World Cup finals in 2019, were squeezed out in South American qualification, but a win on penalties over Venezuela ensured they joined Paraguay in the inter-confederation play-offs.

Hosts India floundered in a Covid-19 ravaged Asian Cup, but alongside the favourites, over-achieving Philippines took their chance. Meanwhile in Africa, Zambia were the surprise qualifiers; with fancied Cameroon and Senegal (who beat Tunisia on penalties) winning through to the inter-confederation play-offs through a best-of-losers mini-tournament. Fiji hosted Oceania's Nations Cup, with New Zealand's absence helping them reach the final, but an always-stronger Papua New Guinea took the trophy and the inter-confederation place.

▶ England's Lauren Hemp takes on Rebecca McKenna of Northern Ireland in a 4-0 victory in the World Cup qualifiying match at Wembley in 2021.

THE HISTORY OF THE WOMEN'S WORLD CUP

INTER-CONFEDERATION PLAY-OFFS

The full draw for the 2023 Women's World Cup groups was not complete until February, when inter-confederation play-offs determined the final three places in the finals. These play-offs also served as a test event for New Zealand, with the seven matches all taking place in either Hamilton or Auckland. For ten teams who had taken part in their federations' qualifying processes, but narrowly missed out, it was a last opportunity to secure a World Cup place.

As the highest-ranked teams, Portugal and Chile automatically qualified for a play-off final. Having beaten Thailand 2-0 in the semi-final in Hamilton, it was Cameroon who faced Portugal. Despite scoring just once, the Europeans were in control throughout the game, only for Cameroon to equalise in the 90th minute. However, a handball four minutes into added-time enabled Carole Costa to slot away the penalty for victory and claim the spot in Group E and a first ever World Cup finals for Portugal.

Meanwhile, in Auckland Haiti handed out a 4-0 thrashing to a disappointing Senegal. Haiti then faced Chile with confidence in the final, where two goals from young superstar Melchie Dumornay put them in front. The South Americans could only muster a single goal in response, so Haiti were off to their first ever World Cup and would play in Group D.

Four teams fought for the final place. In their semi-final against Chinese Taipei, Paraguay found themselves 2-0 down with ten minutes remaining. However, they hauled themselves back to 2-2, were reprieved when Pao missed an extra-time penalty and went on to win the penalty shootout. In the other semi-final, Panama were victorious, beating Papua New Guinea 2-0 after a stunning bicycle kick by Marta Cox opened the scoring. In a tightly fought final over Paraguay, Lineth Cedeño's header late in the second half was enough to deliver victory. A place in Group F for Panama meant all the three winners in the tournament had earned themselves a World Cup debut.

Haiti celebrate World Cup qualification after their 2-1 defeat of Chile in the Inter-Confederation play-off in Auckland, New Zealand.

INTER-CONFEDERATION PLAY-OFFS | MEET THE TEAMS

MEET THE TEAMS

Serial champions, rising challengers, aspirational host nations and underdogs ready to spring a surprise, all whet the appetite for an intriguing tournament. Four-time Women's World Cup winners USA are favourites with Women's EURO 2022 champions England also fancied, but a dozen teams will have serious ambitions of success with the rest eager to make their mark Down Under.

THE HISTORY OF THE WOMEN'S WORLD CUP

GROUP A

All games in this evenly matched group will be played in New Zealand, beginning with the tournament's opening match at Eden Park, Auckland, where the hosts meet Norway.

 New Zealand

 Norway

 Philippines

 Switzerland

MEET THE TEAMS | GROUP A

THE HISTORY OF THE WOMEN'S WORLD CUP

NEW ZEALAND

FIFA WORLD RANKING
25

COLOURS

FIRST | SECOND

NICKNAME: FOOTBALL FRENS

COACH: JITKA KLIMKOVÁ

CAPTAIN: ALI RILEY

BEST WOMEN'S WORLD CUP: GROUP STAGE
(1991, 2007, 2011, 2015, 2019)

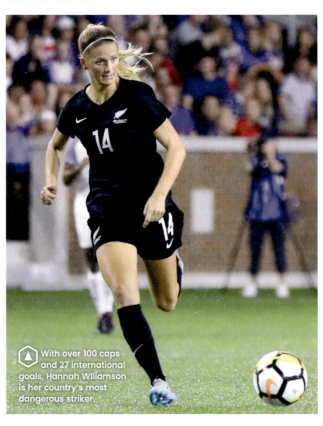

With over 100 caps and 27 international goals, Hannah Wlliamson is her country's most dangerous striker.

ONE TO WATCH: LIV CHANCE

The Celtic midfielder was the Football Ferns' standout player in France 2019 and could well repeat the feat in 2023. With a rare ability to spot a pass and then execute it, all she lacks is the confidence to turn that into a goalscoring opportunity.

As co-hosts, New Zealand enter their fifth successive Women's World Cup still hoping to register their first ever victory in the competition. Their performances have yet to build excitement in Aotearoa (the Māori-language name for New Zealand) and although there are signs of improvement, time is running out for the Football Ferns.

Serious injury to 160-cap Ria Percival and the 'Kiwi Messi', Annalie Longo, as well as the probable (third) retirement of former captain Abby Erceg, have hampered coach Jitka Klimková's preparations. The defence may be well organised with strong options to partner centre-back Claudia Bunge, but the team has struggled to score.

Klimková's hope is that with fit and in-form key players the team can attack with more conviction. She will expect her quality wing-backs, CJ Bott (Leicester City) and Ferns skipper Ali Riley (Angel City in USA), to get forward, while in midfield Liv Chance and, hopefully, a fit Annalie Longo can link up with speedy forward Paige Satchell and leading goalscorer Hannah Williamson. They also have young players who could emerge as stars in the tournament. Riley Indiah-Paige, a 21-year-old right-winger with an eye for goal, was a rising star of the Matildas who recently changed nationality, while two highly rated teenagers in playmaker Alyssa Whinham and striker Milly Clegg have broken into the squad.

New Zealand need the stars to align with players returning to fitness, key figures performing and the team clicking to create a buzz amongst fans, but if they can pull that off, that first victory won't be far away.

GROUP A | NEW ZEALAND AND NORWAY

NORWAY

FIFA WORLD RANKING

12

COLOURS

FIRST   SECOND

NICKNAME: GRASSHOPPERS

COACH: HEGE RIISE

CAPTAIN: MAREN MJELDE

BEST WOMEN'S WORLD CUP: CHAMPIONS (1995)

Will the return of Ada Hegerberg, winner of the inaugural Ballon D'Or Feminin in 2018, inspire the Norwegian team to success?

ONE TO WATCH: CAROLINE GRAHAM HANSEN

At 27, the Barcelona winger has emerged as one of the top players in Europe. Her ability to beat full-backs, move in-field, and reach the byline and cut the ball back is superb, and has made her a leading assist-creator for club and country.

After the nightmare of Women's EURO 2022, when a fancied Norway team endured an 8-0 thrashing by England and crashed out of the tournament, the team quickly had to reset. Who better than Hege Riise, Norway's record appearance-holder and a scorer when the nation lifted the Women's World Cup in 1995, to take over the coaching reins? The former interim England coach has tightened the defence and secured some encouraging results, including a win over the Netherlands and a draw with England.

The return of the great Ada Hegerberg after a five-year absence didn't inspire their Euros, but it has boosted Norway's Women's World Cup qualification campaign, and only a draw in Poland spoiled a 100% record as they scored 47 and let in just two. Hegerberg, six times winner of the Women's Champions League with Lyon, winner of the Ballon D'Or and still one of the best in the world, has formed part of a formidable front three with Barcelona's Caroline Graham Hansen and Chelsea's three-time WSL champion Guro Reiten.

Riise has retained proven players, such as Chelsea's box-to-box midfielder Maren Mjelde, Arsenal's in-form Frida Maanum and Ingrid Engen, an attacking midfielder at Barcelona. She has also continued to develop promising young players with Elisabeth Terland, Celin Bizet and Sophie Haug winning many plaudits, as well as Manchester City's impressive forward, Julie Blakstad.

Can a rejuvenated Norway make up for the disappointment of EURO 2022? With at least two world-class players (Hegerberg and Graham Hansen) and a talented squad, a place in the quarter-finals should be well within reach.

THE HISTORY OF THE WOMEN'S WORLD CUP

PHILIPPINES

FIFA WORLD RANKING

49

COLOURS

FIRST — SECOND

NICKNAME: FILIPINAS

COACH: ALEN STAJCIC

CAPTAIN: TAHNAI ANNIS

BEST WOMEN'S WORLD CUP: FIRST-TIME QUALIFIERS (2023)

ONE TO WATCH: SARINA BOLDEN

With 17 goals in her 29 appearances, including two hat-tricks, the California-born forward has been integral to the Filipinas' meteoric rise. She won the Golden Boot at the 2022 AFF Women's Championship and has been described as the team's 'talisman' by coach Stajcic.

▼ The Filipinas are the first mens or womens team from the Philippines to qualify for the World Cup.

It was the fairy story of the qualifiers. A nation usually fixated on basketball and boxing cheered as their team reach their first Women's World Cup finals – and it was no fluke. Under former Matildas' coach Alen Stajcic, the Filipinas have been on a thrilling journey that saw them win the AFF Championship (for the national teams of Southeast Asia and Australia) for the first time and take the bronze medal in the South East Asian Games, which secured their debut at the World Cup finals.

The youthful Philippines squad – they have an average age around 25 – have been on the up since missing out on the 2019 Women's World Cup in a play-off defeat to South Korea. Since then they have risen over 20 places in the FIFA rankings and, with a team style characterised by discipline and determination, they have defeated Thailand and Vietnam, and earned encouraging draws with Costa Rica and Chile.

The team is led by 34-year-old midfielder Tahnai Annis, with defenders Hali Long and Dominique Randle, and forward Sarina Bolden, among other mainstays of the team. The rest of the squad is largely made up of young Filipino-Americans currently playing US college league soccer and a handful of professionals, including strikers Bolden and Katrina Guillou, who play in the top flight in Japan and Sweden respectively, Serbian league defender Jessika Cowert and impressive midfield anchor Sara Eggesvik, who has played pro-football in England and Norway.

The Filipinas see this tournament as a springboard for women's football in their country. They are on a high and want to go higher, and no one is ready for the fairy tale to end just yet.

GROUP A | PHILIPPINES AND SWITZERLAND

SWITZERLAND

FIFA WORLD RANKING

20

COLOURS

FIRST / SECOND

NICKNAME: ROSSOCROCIATI (RED CROSSES)

COACH: INKA GRINGS

CAPTAIN: LIA WÄLTI

BEST WOMEN'S WORLD CUP: ROUND OF 16 (2015)

Switzerland had an impressive qualification campaign. They scored 44 goals in 10 games and a narrow loss to Italy was their only defeat.

ONE TO WATCH: RIOLA XHEMAILI

One of the squad's brightest stars, the 20-year-old midfielder joined SC Feiburg in 2021 and immediately became a fixture in the German Women's Bundesliga team. A creative player with great technical skill, she has a great assist record and can contribute goals too.

Since qualifying for the 2015 Women's World Cup, Switzerland have succeeded in establishing themselves in the second tier of world football. Their aim now is to compete with the leading nations, although they fell short of that ambition at the Women's EURO 2022 tournament when they didn't make it beyond the group stage. However, 2023 has brought a new coach in the shape of Inka Grings, once a world-class striker for Germany and recently the coach of FC Zürich Frauen, leading them to a league and cup double in her first – and only – season.

While the squad will not have changed significantly, the hope is that Grings can get more out of a talented group of players. Among those playing in Women's Champions League club sides are: composed Arsenal midfield anchor Lia Wälti; her teammate full-back Noelle Maritz; Barcelona winger Ana-Maria Crnogorčević, Switzerland's most prolific goalscorer ever; and forward Ramona Bachmann, who has won league titles with Wolfsburg, Chelsea and PSG.

To make a mark in the Women's World Cup, Switzerland will also look to others to step up. Exciting midfielder Géraldine Reuteler, who shone in the Euros, Svenja Fölmli, a super-talented 20-year-old, whose fast dribbling style has led to comparisons with Kylian Mbappé, and her SC Feiburg teammate, the mercurial Riola Xhemaili all have great potential.

Many eyes will be on Inka Grings' tactical approach and what she can draw from the team. The Swiss will fancy their chances of getting through the group and if the team clicks they could be capable of matching those elite teams.

THE HISTORY OF THE WOMEN'S WORLD CUP

GROUP B

This Australia-based group pitches the co-hosts against high-ranking Canada and two teams capable of a surprise. Canada are group favourites, but they and Ireland face the long trek to Perth.

- 🇦🇺 Australia
- 🇮🇪 Republic of Ireland
- 🇳🇬 Nigeria
- 🇨🇦 Canada

MEET THE TEAMS | GROUP B

THE HISTORY OF THE WOMEN'S WORLD CUP

AUSTRALIA

FIFA WORLD RANKING
10

COLOURS
FIRST / SECOND

NICKNAME: MATILDAS
COACH: TONY GUSTAVSSON
CAPTAIN: SAM KERR
BEST WOMEN'S WORLD CUP: QUARTER-FINALS (2007, 2011, 2015)

▲ An impressive string of performances and results in their long run-up to the World Cup has given the Matildas real belief in their chances of success.

STAR PLAYER: SAM KERR

In 2022 the Chelsea forward was named WSL Footballer of the Year and placed third in the Ballon d'Or. She is fast, skilful and tenacious, as well as having an eye for goal. She has won consecutive Golden Boot awards in the WSL and scored over 60 goals in more than a hundred appearances for her country.

Expectations are high for Women's World Cup co-hosts and three time quarter-finalists, the Matildas – or Tillies. They may be 10th in the world rankings, but they have one of the world's best players, good pre-tournament form and a passionate home crowd to drive them on. Coach Tony Gustavsson, who as an assistant coach twice helped the US team to World Cup glory, is blessed with having his best players at the peak of their careers.

Their world-class skipper Sam Kerr carries many Aussie hopes on her shoulders, but Gustavsson's team is very much made up of big league players. Manchester City winger Hayley Raso and defender Alanna Kennedy are playing the best football of their lives; Arsenal's defender Steph Catley gets better and better; while attacking teammate Caitlin Foord has been rejuvenated by her move to London. Add Olympique Lyonnais' Champions League-winning defender Ellie Carpenter, goalkeeper Mackenzie Arnold (West Ham) and striker Emily van Egmond (San Diego Wave), and the Matildas have proven quality throughout the team.

Not required to qualify as co-hosts, Australia played friendlies against testing opposition. While serious injuries to key players enabled Gustavsson to introduce promising youngsters such as Courtney Nevin, Matilda McNamara, Amy Sayer and Jada Whyman, the team was branded inconsistent. However, since late 2022, as players returned from injury they have put together impressive performances, including victories over Sweden and Denmark. Might they be peaking at just the right time?

GROUP B | AUSTRALIA AND REPUBLIC OF IRELAND

REPUBLIC OF IRELAND

FIFA WORLD RANKING

22

COLOURS

FIRST SECOND

NICKNAME: CAILÍNÍ I NGLAS (GIRLS IN GREEN)

COACH: VERA PAUW

CAPTAIN: KATIE MCCABE

BEST WOMEN'S WORLD CUP: FIRST-TIME QUALIFIERS (2023)

Substitute Amber Barrett had only been on the field four minutes when she scored the play-off winner that took Ireland through to their first major finals. Their qualification reflected a growth in the women's game in Ireland that finally brought professionalism to the Women's National League in December 2022.

Coach Vera Pauw, who took her home country the Netherlands to the Women's EURO 2009 semi-final, has been in charge of the Ireland side since 2019. Fortunate to have players who graduated from the team that reached the semi-final of the 2014 Women's Under-19 Championship, including Katie McCabe, Chloe Mustaki, Savannah McCarthy and Megan Connolly, she has added younger emerging stars.

McCabe takes the captain's armband, but she has experienced heads around her. Now at Liverpool, 35-year-old defender Niamh Fahey has WSL title medals from her time with Arsenal; the tough, towering centre-back Louise Quinn has over 100 caps; and, also approaching a century of appearances, midfielder Denise O'Sullivan has won two NWSL Championships with North Carolina Courage. Joining them are a crop of exciting young players, including teenage sensation Jessie Stapleton and 20-year-old wing-back Jessica Ziu, both at West Ham, and Liverpool's prolific striker Leanne Kiernan, who has recovered from a serious ankle injury.

Despite being drawn in a tough group, they have the experience and quality to surprise more fancied opposition. They have every reason to approach their first major tournament with confidence.

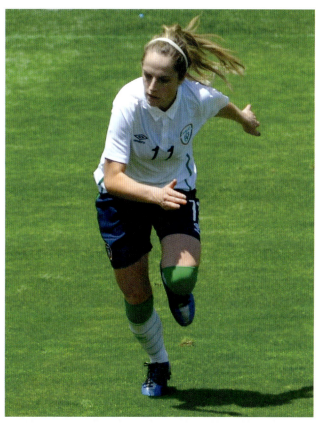

▲ Irish midfielder Julie-Ann Russell spent four years playing in Sydney and will return to the city when the Republic of Ireland meet Australia in their opening group match.

STAR PLAYER: KATIE MCCABE

Named captain of Ireland aged just 21, Katie McCabe is a key player for her country and for Arsenal. Now 27, the left-back turned marauding wing-back provides invaluable assists and goals, and if Ireland are to make progress they will need their 2022 Women's Player of the Year to hit top form.

THE HISTORY OF THE WOMEN'S WORLD CUP

NIGERIA

FIFA WORLD RANKING

42

COLOURS

FIRST   SECOND

NICKNAME: SUPER FALCONS

COACH: RANDY WALDRUM

CAPTAIN: ONOME EBI

BEST WOMEN'S WORLD CUP: QUARTER-FINALS (1999)

Blue haired forward Rasheedat Ajibade is easy to spot, but not so easy to stop.

STAR PLAYER: ASISAT OSHOALA

The current and five-time African Player of the Year scores goals wherever she goes: for Liverpool, Arsenal, Dalian Quanjian in China and now Barcelona. She is a speedy dribbler and packs a powerful shot, so her strikes can be pretty spectacular too.

The Super Falcons are the only African team to qualify for all nine Women's World Cup finals, securing their 2023 World Cup ticket by reaching the semi-finals of the 2023 WAFCON (Women's Africa Cup of Nations) in Morocco. However, defeat in the semi and play-off games, and disappointing performances in subsequent matches, have left coach Randy Waldrum scratching his head and the team low on confidence.

However, the mood could easily change. Any team containing Asisat Oshoala have the potential to be dangerous. One of the world's best, the Barcelona forward is a prolific scorer for club and country, and she is supported by Atlético Madrid's emerging star, the blue-haired, 23-year-old striker Rasheedat Ajibade.

Waldrum may tinker with his team in search of a winning formula, but we can hope to see centre-back and current captain Onome Ebi, who at 40 years old would be playing in her sixth finals; defender Osinachi Ohale; and Chiamaka Nnadozie, the youngest goalkeeper to keep a clean sheet at the Women's World Cup finals and still only 22. Watch out too for Gift Monday, a young forward who has impressed since joining UDG Tenerife, and defender Ashleigh Plumptre, an England Under-23 international, who opted for the Super Eagles and made her debut in the 2022 Women's Africa Cup of Nations.

This is a tough group and Nigeria will have to raise their game to qualify, but if Ajibade and other young talents support the experienced Oshoala, they could be a handful for any team in the tournament.

GROUP B | NIGERIA AND CANADA

CANADA

FIFA WORLD RANKING

6

COLOURS

FIRST   SECOND

NICKNAME: CANUCKS/LES ROUGES (THE REDS)

COACH: BEV PRIESTMAN

CAPTAIN: CHRISTINE SINCLAIR

BEST WOMEN'S WORLD CUP: QUARTER-FINALS (2015)

STAR PLAYER: CHRISTINE SINCLAIR

At the age of 40, 'Sincy' shows little sign of losing her potency in front of goal. Netting five times as she captained the Portland Thorns to a NWSL championship title in 2022, few will bet against her scoring in a record sixth Women's World Cup finals.

Canada will travel to Australia as gold medal winners in the 2020 Olympic Games and finalists in the 2022 CONCACAF W Championship, where they were narrowly defeated by the USA, but which guaranteed their qualification for the World Cup. Over the past year they have also earned draws or beaten top opposition, including USA, England, Germany and Brazil. Canada are a confident team and a force to be reckoned with.

The 2023 Women's World Cup finals will be a swan song for Christine Sinclair, a true legend of women's football. An incredible 189 goals in over 300 appearances make her the all-time highest international goal scorer. Many of the team own a century of caps. They include top-quality players such as goalkeeper Kailen Sheridan, who has shown tremendous form since her move to San Diego Wave, Olympique Lyonnais's Kadeisha Buchanan, one of the world's best defenders; PSG's star full-back Ashley Lawrence and Chelsea's super-creative midfielder Jessie Fleming.

Priestman has built an attacking team, who enjoy possession and press high up the field. Her full-backs push forward with holding midfielders Disiree Scott and Quinn (the first openly trans, non-binary Olympic medallist) allowing Fleming to get forward. Up front, Sinclair often drops back to pull strings, with Nichelle Prince or Jordan Huitema providing the firepower.

Canada will have to be at their strongest to beat the world's best, but how the Olympic champions would love another chance of glory.

THE HISTORY OF THE WOMEN'S WORLD CUP

GROUP C

Spain and Japan are likely to be the nations that progress from four teams battling it out in New Zealand, and they will meet in the final group game.

- 🇪🇸 **Spain**
- 🇨🇷 **Costa Rica**
- 🇿🇲 **Zambia**
- 🇯🇵 **Japan**

MEET THE TEAMS | GROUP C

THE HISTORY OF THE WOMEN'S WORLD CUP

SPAIN

FIFA WORLD RANKING

7

COLOURS

FIRST / SECOND

NICKNAME: LA ROJA / LAS SOÑADORAS

COACH: JORGE VILDA

CAPTAIN: ALEXIA PUTELLAS

BEST WOMEN'S WORLD CUP: ROUND OF 16 (2019)

STAR PLAYER: AITANA BONMATI

With Putellas' fitness in doubt the spotlight falls on her Barcelona partner. Bonmati was already conducting play in the style of male compatriot Iniesta, but had added a goalscoring threat to her driving runs to put her among the world's elite.

Spain should be among the tournament favourites, yet they have some major issues. First, there is the fitness of the world's best player, the 2021 and 2022 Ballon d'Or winner, Alexia Putellas, who has been injured since last summer. Second, there is an ongoing dispute with the methods of coach Jorge Vilda, which saw many senior players withdraw from the squad in autumn 2022, including top quality defenders Irene Paredes of Barcelona, club colleague Mapi León and Manchester United's Ona Batile.

Midfielder Putellas is the complete player; a consummate passer and dribbler, and a deadly free-kick specialist. For Barcelona and Spain she forms a mesmerising partnership with midfield pivot Patri Guijarro and the masterful Aitana Bonmati. Add their teammate Mariona Cladentey and young Real Madrid winger Athenea del Castillo and you have an attacking force the envy of any team in the tournament.

Spain play tiki-taka possession with quick interchanges of passing and like to exert an intense press. They can be susceptible at the back though, as seen in their defeats to Germany and England at the Euros (where they missed Putellas and all-time top scorer Jennifer Hermoso).

They have great talent within the squad and could easily negotiate a route through to the later rounds, but that is set against the problems they must overcome before July, so there is just one word that sums up Spain's World Cup prospects: intriguing.

◀ The ongoing dispute could lead to Spain fielding a young and untested team at the World Cup.

GROUP C | SPAIN AND COSTA RICA

COSTA RICA

FIFA WORLD RANKING

36

COLOURS

FIRST / SECOND

NICKNAME: LAS TIKAS

COACH: AMELIA VALVERDE

CAPTAIN: KATHERINE ALVARADO

BEST WOMEN'S WORLD CUP: GROUP STAGE (2015)

Costa Rican women have had fairly limited success on the international football stage. However, in their sole Women's World Cup outing, in 2015, they secured two surprising draws – with Spain and South Korea – and only went out after losing to Brazil. Qualification this time came through a fourth place in the 2022 CONCACAF W Championship, after wins over Panama, and Trinidad and Tobago.

This team will be hoping to spring some surprises themselves. They will approach the tournament in the same way that they set out their stall in the CONCACAF Championships, playing a defensive 5-4-1 with just Raquel Rodriguez up front. In the 2023 Revelations Cup in Mexico, this approach earned them a draw with the hosts and Colombia and a narrow defeat to Nigeria.

At the heart of the team are players who enjoyed that 2015 campaign, including midfielder Katherine Alvarado, defender Lixy Rodríguez, who plays for Leon in Mexico, and Costa Rica's long-standing star, playmaker Shirley Cruz. Now 37, she won six league titles and two Women's Champions League finals with Lyon between 2006 and 2012. Some of the younger players also bring international experience. Raquel Rodríguez is at Portland Thorns and skilful winger Priscila Chinchilla is impressing for Glasgow City, while defender Stephanie Blanco plays for Sporting de Huelva in Spain's top league.

Costa Rica will be out to recreate those 2015 shocks, but that will only happen if they maintain a disciplined defence and find a way for their skilful midfield to create some magic.

Shirley Cruz was the star of Costa Rica's 2015 finals, but Las Tikas still rely on the creative skills of their veteran playmaker.

STAR PLAYER: RAQUEL RODRÍGUEZ

'Rocky' scored Costa Rica's first ever Women's World Cup goal in the 2015 draw with Spain and has scored over 40 more since. Dynamic and strong on the ball, the midfielder was an integral part of Portland Thorns' 2022 championship-winning side.

THE HISTORY OF THE WOMEN'S WORLD CUP

FIFA WORLD RANKING
77

COLOURS

FIRST — SECOND

NICKNAME: COPPER QUEENS

COACH: BRUCE MWAPE

CAPTAIN: BARBRA BANDA

BEST WOMEN'S WORLD CUP: FIRST-TIME QUALIFIERS (2023)

ONE TO WATCH: BARBRA BANDA

Still only 23, Banda is already the team's captain and inspiration. The strong and immensely skilful forward missed some international matches due to gender eligibility issues, but is now cleared to play and has the potential to become one of the world's best.

The Copper Queens' most successful era ever began with their first Olympic Games qualification in 2020 where, despite a 10-3 reverse against the Netherlands, they emerged with a credible draw with China and a narrow defeat by Brazil. They followed this in 2022 by winning their first ever COSAFA Women's Championship (for southern African countries) and third place – their best ever performance – at WAFCON (Women's Africa Cup of Nations), a result which sent them to their first ever Women's World Cup finals.

The rise has been steered by coach Bruce Mwape, who took the helm in 2018. He has taken full advantage of players making a name for themselves overseas or with the Green Buffaloes, the first Zambian team to compete in the CAF Women's Champions League. These include goalkeeper Hazel Nali and right-back Margaret Belemu, both of whom play in Turkey, and the Buffaloes' experienced defensive pairing of Agness Musase and Lushomo Mweemba.

It is, however, their attacking force that promises to excite in New Zealand. The Spain-based trio of midfielder Rachael Nachula, playmaker Grace Chanda and forward Rachael Kundananji are supported by explosive winger Xiomara Mapepa, who was 2022 top scorer in the Spanish National League, and the 'Female Computer' Irene Lungu, who pulls the strings in midfield. Above all, they have Barbra Banda, who illuminated the Olympics with back-to-back hat-tricks, then impressed after a big-money move to Shanghai Shengli.

Zambia face a massive battle to progress from a very competitive group, but win or lose, with such exciting attacking players they will certainly be worth watching in New Zealand.

▲ Among the first nations to qualify for the World Cup, the Copper Queens are a team on the rise.

GROUP C | ZAMBIA AND JAPAN

JAPAN

FIFA WORLD RANKING
11

COLOURS
FIRST / SECOND

NICKNAME: NADESHIKO JAPAN
COACH: FUTOSHI IKEDA
CAPTAIN: SAKI KUMAGAI
BEST WOMEN'S WORLD CUP: CHAMPIONS (2011)

A right back who loves to attack, Risa Shimizu has settled in well in the WSL with West Ham United.

Becoming World Champions in 2011 was a momentous achievement for Japan and the subsequent triumph in the 2014 Asian Cup and narrow defeats to USA in both the 2012 Olympic Games and 2015 Women's World Cup finals proved Japan were a force in world football. Unfortunately, in the subsequent years, the Nadeshiko were unable to maintain that position and have slipped out of the world's top ten ranked nations.

The feeling among many in the game is that Japan should be closer to the top nations. After all, coach Futoshi Ikeda has a squad full of talent from the world's top leagues. His team will be built around 2011 Women's World Cup winners Saki Kumagi and Arsenal's tricky Mana Iwabuchi, along with in-form midfielders Hina Sugita of Portland Thorns and Manchester City's star Yui Hasegawa, with consistent goalscorer Mina Tanaka of Bayer Leverkusen up front.

Utilising these technically gifted players, Ikeda favours a style that relies on possession and clever passing to create changes rather than individual skill. However, defeats to Spain and England in friendlies in November suggest he is still tinkering with formations and the line-up in an attempt to get the team firing. That means much may depend on how successfully he integrates younger players, such as striker Riko Ueki, midfielder Fuka Nagano and defender Nanami Kitamura from the 2018 Under-20 Women's World Cup winning team, or even recent Chelsea signing Maika Hamano, whose goals helped Japan reach the final of the Under-20 Women's World Cup in 2022.

ONE TO WATCH: YUI HASEGAWA

The 26-year-old midfielder helped Nippon TV Beleza win five consecutive league titles before impressing at AC Milan, West Ham and now Manchester City. A naturally creative player, City use her in a more defensive role while retaining her attacking threat, a development that could prove invaluable to Nadeshiko Japan.

THE HISTORY OF THE WOMEN'S WORLD CUP

GROUP D

Reigning Women's EURO Champions England are favourites to top this Australia-based group, but Denmark's meeting with China out in west-coast Perth will be perhaps the most intriguing of the matches.

 England

 Haiti

Denmark

China

MEET THE TEAMS | GROUP D

43

THE HISTORY OF THE WOMEN'S WORLD CUP

ENGLAND

FIFA WORLD RANKING

4

COLOURS

FIRST · SECOND

NICKNAME: LIONESSES

COACH: SARINA WIEGMAN

CAPTAIN: LEAH WILLIAMSON

BEST WOMEN'S WORLD CUP: THIRD PLACE (2011)

Having reached the semi-finals at the past two Women's World Cup tournaments, England will be hoping to go one better in 2023. As champions of the EURO 2022 they travel to this tournament on a high.

Sarina Wiegman, who led Netherlands to the 2019 Women's World Cup final, became England coach in 2021. She transformed the team and won every World Cup qualifier and EURO 2022 match, adopting a pragmatic and flexible approach. Wiegman's only issues are the retirement of midfield stalwart Jill Scott and record goalscorer Ellen White, and injury doubts over star striker Beth Mead.

However, the squad has enough quality to sustain such blows. In front of the increasingly impressive Mary Earps in goal, the settled defence features Chelsea's Millie Bright and Barcelona's Lucy Bronze, both of whom were nominated for the 2022 Ballon D'Or. Bronze's teammate Keira Walsh, who many thought should have made that list, orchestrates a midfield that is full of creative talent with Ella Toone, Fran Kirby and Georgia Stanway all attacking threats. Strikers Alessia Russo and Chloe Kelly, so effective as substitutes in the Euros, will be ready to fill the gaps up front, supported by the brilliant Lauren Hemp.

If anyone can bring the best out of an already top-class team it is Sarina Wiegman and England will travel to Australia (where they will play all their games) knowing that this is their best ever chance of glory.

ONE TO WATCH: LAUREN HEMP

Voted PFA Women's Young Player of the Year for the fourth time in 2022, the Manchester City left-winger has added goals to her ability to run at defenders and cut in from the flanks, and is improving with every game.

Euro 2022 Champions, England travel Down Under as one of the tournament favourites.

GROUP D | ENGLAND AND HAITI

HAITI

FIFA WORLD RANKING

53

COLOURS

FIRST / SECOND

NICKNAME: THE GRENADIERS

COACH: NICOLAS DELÉPINE

CAPTAIN: NÉRILIA MONDÉSIR

BEST WOMEN'S WORLD CUP: FIRST-TIME QUALIFIERS (2023)

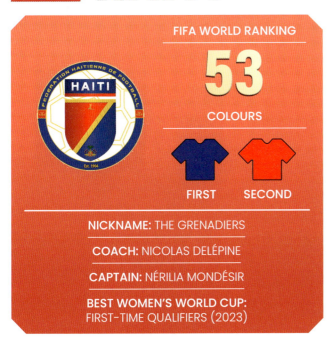

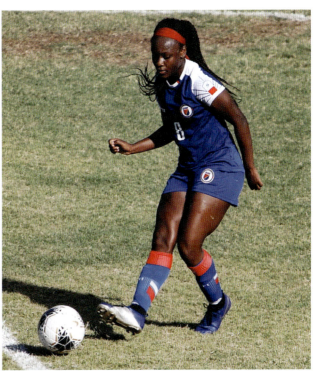

American-born midfielder Danielle Étienne has represented for Haiti at every age level. She has scored for the Under-17, Under-19 and Under-20 national teams, but awaits her first senior goal.

STAR PLAYER: MELCHIE DUMORNAY

The 2022 winner of the prestigious NXGN Best Teenage Player in the World award, the 19-year-old midfielder known as "Corventina" has physicality, pace and great technical skill. A regular scorer for Reims for two seasons, she has now joined Lyon and seems destined for greatness.

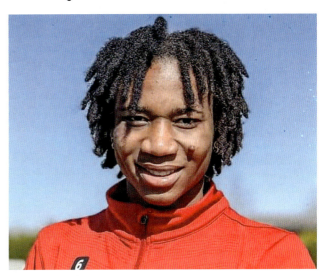

Haiti registered the shock of the February inter-confederation play-offs when they beat Chile to book a place in their first ever Women's World Cup finals. It was a welcome source of joy for a country still suffering from the apocalyptic 2010 earthquake, a presidential assassination and a spiralling humanitarian crisis.

The Grenadiers' play-offs thrashing of Senegal, and the narrow victory over a Chilean team ranked 20 places above them, followed impressive 2022 defeats of Costa Rica and Mexico (and a 21-0 victory over the British Virgin Islands!). This highlights that there is the spirit and talent in the Haiti team to make it capable of achieving such an upset. On the other hand, recent heavy defeats to USA, Portugal and Jamaica should caution against over-excitement.

Haiti have one of the youngest squads at the finals with most players in their early 20s and many, including defenders Kethna Louis and Claire Constant, playing for teams in the top leagues in France. They may set out in a solid 4-5-1 formation, but, as several opponents have discovered, they have plenty of players able to get forward quickly. Among them are captain Nérilia Mondésir, a striker for Montpelier who has earned the nickname "Nérigol"; Dijon's versatile Roselord Borgella; the speedy Sherly Jeudy; and wonder girl Melchie Dumornay, whose two goals sank Chile in the play-offs.

Finding themselves in one of the toughest possible groups, Haiti are going to have to conjure up something special just to take home a point, but they won't be short of support from neutrals, willing them on to do just that.

45

THE HISTORY OF THE WOMEN'S WORLD CUP

DENMARK

FIFA WORLD RANKING

15

COLOURS

FIRST | SECOND

NICKNAME: DE RØD-HVIDE (RED AND WHITE)

COACH: LARS SØNDERGAARD

CAPTAIN: PERNILLE HARDER

BEST WOMEN'S WORLD CUP: QUARTER-FINAL (1991, 1995)

Denmark's experienced defender Simone Sørensen (5) holds off Austria's Nicole Billa.

As EURO 2017 finalists, Denmark's failure to qualify for the following year's Women's World Cup was a disappointment. However, the squad reacted well, putting up a spirited show in a tough EURO 2022 group and romped through qualification for the 2023 finals. Coach since 2017, Lars Søndergaard has them playing attractive, often high-scoring, football, getting plenty of players in the box as the wing-backs provide dangerous crosses.

Chelsea's superb attacking midfielder, Pernille Harder, is the team's danger player. Denmark's chances rely heavily on her full recovery from a serious hamstring injury, but they are not lacking in other talent. Goalkeeper Lene Christensen was a star in EURO 2022, and they have former Arsenal and Bayern Munich centre-back Simone Sørensen and hard-tackling Stine Ballisager in defence.

Further forward, Denmark boast Juventus' box-to-box midfielder Sofie Junge, Arsenal's 2023 signing Kathrine Kühl, who is heralded as one of the world's best young players, and the flying powerhouse that is Real Madrid's wing-back, Sofie Svava. She is a strong defender who could emerge as a tournament star.

The squad also includes Sofie Bredgaard, another youngster with massive potential; Signe Bruun, a league winner with PSG who is now at Lyon; and legend Nadia Nadim, the 34-year-old with over 100 caps and approaching 40 goals for her country. And then there's Pernille Harder, a brilliant leader, creator and scorer who will hopefully pick up the brilliant form she displayed at Chelsea before her injury.

STAR PLAYER: PERNILLE HARDER

The most expensive female footballer in the world, the Chelsea star was at her best, scoring six goals in as many games, when a hamstring injury led to surgery in November 2022. With flair, vision and an ease on the ball, a fit and in-form Harder will be difficult to stop.

GROUP D | DENMARK AND CHINA

CHINA

FIFA WORLD RANKING
13

COLOURS
FIRST SECOND

NICKNAME: STEEL ROSES
COACH: SHUI QINGXIA
CAPTAIN: WU HAIYAN
BEST WOMEN'S WORLD CUP: RUNNER-UP (1999)

China have a long-term plan to win the Women's World Cup in 2035 with a quarter-final place in 2023 as the first step. That is a feat they have achieved on six previous occasions, having qualified for every finals apart from 2011 and having never failed to get out of the group stage. It seemed unlikely after their dismal performance at the Olympic Games in summer 2021, but new coach Shui Qingxia worked wonders – with their first Women's Asia Cup victory in 15 years came World Cup qualification and the team remained unbeaten throughout 2022.

China have the players to give a good account of themselves at the finals. Striker Wang Shuang is a household name in China and an inspiration to the team, and other players are finally playing in top European leagues. In 2022 defender Li Mengwen and midfielder Yang Lina both joined PSG on a season-long loan, while Zhang Linyan, a forward who was a star in the Asia Cup, joined Grasshopper Club Zurich. Tang Jiali, a winger with a great goalscoring record, spent a season at Tottenham Hotspur and is now at Real Madrid, while at just 21 years-old Shen Mengyu has impressed with her assured and tireless performances in midfield for Celtic in the Scottish Women's Premier League.

The chances of China repeating their 1999 achievement when they lost the final in a penalty shoot-out are unlikely and even the quarter-final target seems ambitious. However, the team has prepared well. Shui Qingxia has created a well-organised team with attacking talent who might yet surprise the more fancied teams.

▲ China's midfielder Zhang Rui (20) tracks Australia's Caitlin Foord. Rui has over 150 caps to her name.

ONE TO WATCH: WANG SHUANG

The 2018 Asian Women's Player of the Year is still only 28 years old and is the fulcrum of the China team. A midfielder with a magic left foot, Wang Shuang has played for PSG and now stars for Racing Louisville in the NWSL.

47

THE HISTORY OF THE WOMEN'S WORLD CUP

GROUP E

New Zealand host a group in which a rematch of the 2019 final between USA and the Netherlands in Wellington will be the main focus.

 USA

 Vietnam

 Netherlands

 **Portugal**

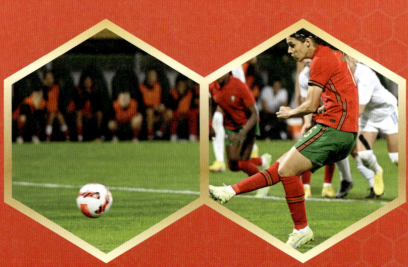

MEET THE TEAMS | GROUP E

THE HISTORY OF THE WOMEN'S WORLD CUP

USA

FIFA WORLD RANKING: 1

COLOURS
FIRST / SECOND

NICKNAME: STARS AND STRIPES
COACH: VLATKO ANDONOVSKI
CAPTAIN: BECKY SAUERBRUNN
BEST WOMEN'S WORLD CUP: CHAMPIONS (1991, 1999, 2015, 2019)

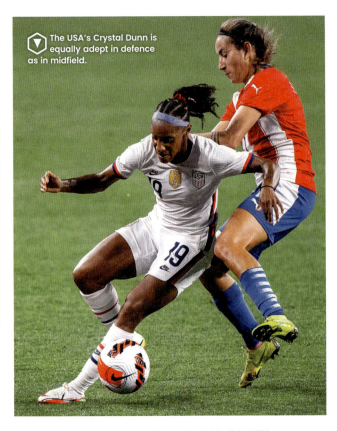

The USA's Crystal Dunn is equally adept in defence as in midfield.

USA will travel to the Women's World Cup finals as joint favourites to win their third straight title (or as they say, a 'three-peat'). They are the top-ranked team in the world and coach Andonovski's biggest headache is who to select from a squad brimming full of quality.

After having had to settle for bronze medal at the 2020 Olympic Games, and prompted by injuries to senior players, Andonovski successfully brought in a number of young players. Most eye-catching of these were Naomi Girma, an astonishingly composed defender, lightning-paced winger Trinity Rodman (daughter of basketball legend, Dennis) and Portland Thorns' sensational forward Sophia Smith.

These strengthened a squad that already boasted Mallory Swanson (née Pugh), Chicago Red Star's ever-dangerous winger, and Lyon midfielder Lindsey Horan, the US Female Player of the Year in 2021, as well as the return from injury of rising star Catarina Macario, an attacking player whose ability to drop deep gives Andonovski more options. None of which overshadows the quality of veterans like defender Becky Sauerbrunn, versatile midfielder Rose Lavelle, the rejuvenated, goal-hungry Alex Morgan and inspirational Megan Rapinhoe, at 38 still capable of a game-changing cameo.

Such wealth of talent might imply the trophy is as good as won. However, as friendly defeats to England and Spain in late 2022 showed, USA are beatable. They play an effective high press, high-energy game and attack with speed, which can be countered by well-organised teams. Make no mistake though: this is the team all others will fear most.

ONE TO WATCH: SOPHIA SMITH

The 22-year old winger and occasional centre-forward was named the NWSL's Most Valuable Player in 2022. She appears to be the complete package, yet continues to reveal new facets to her game. A good World Cup could see her become one of the world's best even sooner than expected.

GROUP E | USA AND VIETNAM

VIETNAM

FIFA WORLD RANKING
33

COLOURS

FIRST / SECOND

NICKNAME: GOLDEN STAR WOMEN WARRIORS

COACH: MAI ĐỨC CHUNG

CAPTAIN: HUỲNH NHƯ

BEST WOMEN'S WORLD CUP: RUNNER-UP (1999)

Vietnam will need concentration, energy and some tenacious defending to match their opponents in a fiercely tough group.

ONE TO WATCH: HUỲNH NHƯ

Named Vietnam's Player of the Year on four occasions and scorer of over 60 goals for her country, Như is already becoming a legend at home. If given an opportunity to show her speed, skill and eye for goal, she could have a tournament to remember.

Vietnam travel to New Zealand buoyed by the support of a football-mad nation who are seeing their first representatives, male or female, at a World Cup finals. Despite being the best team in the region and winning the gold medal in the last three South East Asia games, Vietnam have failed to translate that success to a larger arena. It was, however, a fifth place in the AFC Women's Asian Cup in 2022, their best ever finish, which won the nation a place at their first Women's World Cup.

With only one of their number playing abroad, the squad is taken from the leading clubs of the as-yet non-professional Vietnamese League. Goalkeeper Kim Thanh, stand-out defender Chuong Thi Kieu and the skilful Bich Thuy, who can play on either wing, are all from Vietnam's top club Ho Chi Min City, while the experienced Tuyết Dung of Phong Phú Hà Nam partners the country's Best Young Female Player, Ngân Thị Vạn Sự, in midfield.

At the front of what is usually a 3–5–2 formation is the dangerous pairing of Hanoi's prolific scorer Phạm H'ai Yến and captain Huỳnh Như, who became Vietnam's first overseas female footballer when she signed for the Portuguese club Vilaverdense.

With USA and The Netherlands in their group, Vietnam will be hoping to get a result against Portugal and cause a seismic shock against one of those super-nations. They might only have a wafer-thin chance, but will be sure of thousands at home willing them to pull off their greatest ever result.

THE HISTORY OF THE WOMEN'S WORLD CUP

NETHERLANDS

FIFA WORLD RANKING

8

COLOURS

FIRST / SECOND

NICKNAME: ORANJELEEUWINNEN (ORANGE LIONESSES)

COACH: ANDRIES JONKER

CAPTAIN: SHERIDA SPITSE

BEST WOMEN'S WORLD CUP: RUNNERS-UP (2019)

Liverpool and Netherlands winger Shanice van de Sanden evades Elise Thorsnes of Norway.

STAR PLAYER: LIEKE MARTENS

Seemingly capable of creating and scoring at will, the winger left Barcelona, where she had won a bucketful of medals, for PSG in 2022. Injury ruined her Euros, but if she can find form she can light up this tournament.

As the Women's EURO 2017 champions and 2019 Women's World Cup finalists, it seemed the Netherlands had established themselves among the elite in women's football. However, coach Sarina Wiegman departed after a disappointing 2020 Olympic Games and replacement Mark Parsons' highly rated team flopped in EURO 2022. Then new coach Andries Jonker immediately faced a must-win match against Iceland in the 2023 Women's World Cup qualifiers, which the Netherlands only won in stoppage time.

Jonker has used subsequent friendlies to experiment with tactics, trying 3–5–2 rather than the traditional 4–3–3 and integrating PSV's promising teenager Esmee Brugts, scorer of that crucial goal against Iceland. Then came a huge blow. In December 2022 a horrendous ACL injury robbed him of the world-class services of Arsenal's three-time Ballon D'Or nominated striker and Oranje leading goalscorer Vivianne Miedema, who will now miss the finals.

Nevertheless, Jonker can choose from a squad drawn from Europe's top sides. Wolfsburg's defensive pairing of Lynn Wilms and Dominique Janssen, along with holding midfielders Sherida Spitse and former Arsenal and now Lyon star Daniëlle Van de Donk, can shield impressive young keeper Daphne van Domselaar from Twente. Going forward, it will be down to Esmee Brugts, Wolfsburg playmaker Jill Roord and former Barcelona winger Lieke Martens to create and score, with Juventus's Lineth Beerensteyn and Twente's prolific goalscorer Fenna Kalma among the strikers expected to fill Miedema's golden boots.

The Netherlands match against USA in Wellington is one of the most eagerly anticipated of the group games and should show if Jonker has a team that will find success down under.

GROUP E | NETHERLANDS AND PORTUGAL

PORTUGAL

FIFA WORLD RANKING

21

COLOURS

FIRST / SECOND

NICKNAME: SELECÇÃO DAS QUINAS (TEAM OF THE CASTLES)

COACH: FRANCISCO NETO

CAPTAIN: DOLORES SILVA

BEST WOMEN'S WORLD CUP: FIRST-TIME QUALIFIERS (2023)

Carole Costa coolly converts an extra-time penalty to help Portugal progress through the Women's World Cup qualifying play-off rounds.

ONE TO WATCH: KIKA NAZARETH

At just 20 years old, this skilful, attacking midfielder has already scored six international goals and is the most promising women's player Portugal have ever produced. Currently playing at Benfica, if she showcases her talents Down Under, a big move may be imminent.

Carole Costa's cool-as-you-like penalty in the fourth minute of added-on time in their inter-confederation play-off against Cameroon completed a remarkable and dramatic qualification for Portugal. Their victory followed a last-gasp winner over Belgium and an extra-time victory over Iceland in previous play-off rounds. They are a team who like to leave it late.

Portugal's first Women's World Cup finals follows appearances at two consecutive European Championships, in 2017 and 2022. When coach Francisco Neto took over in 2014 they were ranked 42nd in the world and have since climbed 20 places. In Euro 2022 they drew with Switzerland and narrowly lost to the Netherlands, considering themselves unlucky on both occasions, while only Germany managed to defeat them in World Cup qualification.

Coach Neto likes to play a solid 4-4-2 or 3-4-3 and remains loyal, making few changes to his squad. He has established a strong base of players, who include central defender Carole Costa, the Portuguese League's Player of the Season in 2022, and midfielder Dolores Silva, a league winner with Atlético Madrid. The wide positions are served by Sporting CP's Ana Borges, who has won the FA Cup and WSL with Chelsea, and her teammate, the tricky winger Diana Silva, while Jéssica Silva, a Champions League winner at Lyon, or veteran striker Carolina Mendes, provide the goal threat. Portugal have shown the application and quality to beat teams ranked close to them, but now they face the world's best.

THE HISTORY OF THE WOMEN'S WORLD CUP

GROUP F

Quite a few teams will be watching to see just how good France and Brazil really are when they meet in Brisbane and play out a seemingly easy group across Australia.

🇫🇷 **France**

🇯🇲 **Jamaica**

🇧🇷 **Brazil**

🇵🇦 **Panama**

MEET THE TEAMS | GROUP F

55

THE HISTORY OF THE WOMEN'S WORLD CUP

FRANCE

FIFA WORLD RANKING

5

COLOURS

FIRST / SECOND

NICKNAME: LES BLEUES

COACH: HERVÉ RENARD

CAPTAIN: WENDIE RENARD

BEST WOMEN'S WORLD CUP: SEMI-FINAL (2011)

▶ Lyon's 22-year-old Selma Bacha is arguably the best left-back in the world, but often plays as a winger for the national side.

ONE TO WATCH:
MARIE-ANTOINETTE KATOTO

How France missed their super-striker when a serious knee injury ruled her out of the Euros. An explosive sprinter and deadly in front of goal, the 24-year-old is already PSG's all-time top scorer and has 26 goals in 32 appearances for France. They will be praying for her return to fitness.

As 2019 Women's World Cup hosts and at EURO 2022, Les Bleues were eventually found wanting, losing to eventual winner's USA in a quarter-final and hitting the brick wall that was Germany in the EURO 2022 semi-final. Former Saudi Arabia men's team coach Hervé Renard was appointed coach in March 2023 in a bid to prevent a full-scale mutiny by players against former coach Diacre. Hopefully, their key players will be present at the finals.

Having adjusted to life without former captain Amandine Henry, top scorer Eugénie Le Sommer and others, France appear to be a close-knit squad. New generation stars Marie-Antoinette Katoto, one of Europe's elite goalscorers, and the attacking pairing of Lyon's Delphine Cascarino, a winger whose pace and dribbling bamboozles defenders, and the powerful and fast Kadidiatou Diani from PSG, have settled in alongside experienced holding midfielder Grace Geyoro; Sakina Karchaoui, a complete full-back; and the ever reliable skipper, central defender Wendie Renard.

France can also call on exciting youngsters such as Lyon's Selma Bacha, arguably the best left-back in the world, and 20-year-old Melvine Malard, who has taken advantage of Katoto's absence through injury to show her predatory attributes in front of goal. Meanwhile, PSG midfielder, Laurina Fazer, the French 2022 Young Player of the Year, and Real Madrid's Naomie Feller, touted as one of the brightest attacking talents in Europe, have both received regular squad call-ups.

With autumn friendly defeats to Germany and Sweden, doubts resurfaced over France's ability to overcome the top nations. However, with a team of great talent augmented by a fully recovered Kakoto, France should not be underestimated.

GROUP F | FRANCE AND JAMAICA

JAMAICA

FIFA WORLD RANKING

43

COLOURS

FIRST   SECOND

NICKNAME: REGGAE GIRLZ

COACH: LORNE DONALDSON

CAPTAIN: KHADIJA SHAW

BEST WOMEN'S WORLD CUP: GROUP STAGE (2019)

The Reggae Girlz team spirit (along with Bunny Shaw's goals) have helped take them on an exciting journey. It is one they won't want to end too soon.

When Jamaica qualified for the 2019 Women's World Cup it was heralded as an astounding feat. Yet the finals themselves dealt a hard lesson with heavy defeats at the hands of Brazil, Italy and Australia. In 2023, they say, it will be different...

And they have good reason to believe. Qualification from a CONCACAF Women's Championship group containing USA, Mexico and an in-form Haiti was again against the odds, but after a surprise victory over Mexico they never looked back. During 2022 they rose from 51 to 43 in the FIFA world rankings and backed by ambassador Cedella Marley, daughter of reggae legend Bob Marley, coach Lorne Donaldson has prepared thoroughly with training camps and tough international friendlies.

Many of his squad have World Cup finals experience and his key players play in top leagues. In Manchester City centre-forward Khadija Shaw they have a world-class forward, a natural leader and Jamaica's all-time top goalscorer. She was instrumental in the qualification campaign, but was ably supported by midfielder Drew Spence, a Chelsea legend now at Tottenham Hotspur, and Florida State Seminoles forward Jody Brown.

The Reggae Girlz are a well-organised unit with sisters Allyson and Chantellle Swaby marshalling the defence and Havana Solaun patrolling as a holding midfielder. However, for all their attacking talent, their finishing has let them down in recent matches and will need to improve if they are really to better their last World Cup adventure.

STAR PLAYER: KHADIJA SHAW

'Bunny' as she is universally known is a tall, strong forward who uses her physicality and skill to create and score. After chalking up nearly a goal a game over two seasons for Bordeaux, she joined Manchester City in 2021 and now features among the WSL's leading goalscorers.

57

THE HISTORY OF THE WOMEN'S WORLD CUP

BRAZIL

FIFA WORLD RANKING

9

COLOURS

FIRST — SECOND

NICKNAME: AS CANARINHAS (CANARIES)

COACH: PIA SUNDHAGE

CAPTAIN: MARTA

BEST WOMEN'S WORLD CUP: RUNNER-UP (2007)

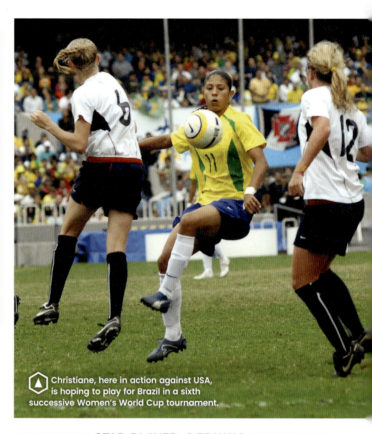

Christiane, here in action against USA, is hoping to play for Brazil in a sixth successive Women's World Cup tournament.

What promised to be a golden era for Brazil has come to a close without Olympic gold or a World Cup win. The three legends – Marta, Formiga and Christiane – have lit up tournaments since 2007, but as Marta said in her passionate speech after Brazil's elimination from the 2019 Women's World Cup, it is time for a new generation to step up.

Pia Sundhage, one of Sweden's greatest ever players and an experienced coach, took over after the 2019 finals and has made steady progress. A quarter-final defeat on penalties to eventual winners Canada in the 2020 Olympic Games was followed by a 2022 Copa América triumph in which they won every game without conceding a goal.

Marta has been battling a long-term injury, but if she fails to find her fitness Sundhage can still call upon experienced players. Stand-in captain Rafaelle effortlessly eased into the centre of Arsenal's defence in 2022; left-back Corinthians' Tamires is playing in her third finals; and Kansas City Current's Debhina, with over 50 goals for her country, leads the forward line. Meanwhile, Marta's mantle has been taken up by Orlando Pride forward Adriana, Geyse, who hit such goalscoring form at Madrid CFF that she was snapped up by Barcelona in 2022, and Kerolin, her striking partner in the Spanish capital, whose pace and dazzling feet earned her a move to North Carolina Courage, also in 2022.

Brazil are still the powerhouse of South American women's football, and they have the coach and players to take on USA and the elite European nations. The trophy might still elude them, but they're definitely capable of getting close.

STAR PLAYER: **DEBHINA**

Marta might still grab the attention, but there is no ignoring the extravagantly skilled forward Debhina, a star at North Carolina Courage who joined Kansas City Current in 2023. Her dribbling and magic footwork make her a joy to watch and a constant threat anywhere near goal.

GROUP F | BRAZIL AND PANAMA

PANAMA

FIFA WORLD RANKING

52

COLOURS

FIRST — SECOND

NICKNAME: LAS CANALERAS (THE CANAL GIRLS)

COACH: IGNACIO QUINTANA

CAPTAIN: MARTA COX

BEST WOMEN'S WORLD CUP: FIRST-TIME QUALIFIERS (2023)

ONE TO WATCH: RILEY TANNER

A pacy left-sided forward who makes and scores goals, Riley Tanner impressed in the inter-confederation play-offs. She moved to the United States when she was four-years old and became the first Panamanian in the NWSL when she joined Washington Spirit in 2023.

Despondent after losing out on a place in the 2019 Women's World Cup finals after a penalty shoot-out against Jamaica, Panama's victory over Paraguay in the 2023 inter-confederation play-offs was wildly celebrated, and reflected the confidence and ability of a team who have shown significant improvement over the past five years.

In the 2018 CONCACAF Championship, the tournament for North and Central American and Caribbean teams, their fourth place in 2018 was Las Canaleras' best-ever placing, while 2022 saw them fall to just a narrow defeat by highly rated Canada.

Coach Ignacio Quintana has assembled a young squad who mainly play in Panama or neighbouring Costa Rica. Defender Rosario Vargas and Lineth Cedeño, scorer of the momentous winner against Paraguay, both play in Europe, while Quintana has also turned to talented US-born players in full-back Carina Baltrip-Reyes and forward Gabriela Villagrand.

Much of Panama's attacking play is instigated by the team's captain and scorer of an acrobatic bicycle kick in the play-offs, Martha Cox. Among the other leading names are striker Riley Tanner and keeper Yenith Bailey, who converted from a midfielder to goalkeeper in 2017, and won the Golden Glove award at the 2018 CONCACAF Women's Championship. Las Canaleras are savouring the chance to play in the World Cup finals, but are realistic about the challenges they face against the three high-quality teams in the group.

Having reached the finals against the odds, Panama's young team have nothing to lose in Australia.

THE HISTORY OF THE WOMEN'S WORLD CUP

GROUP G

Sweden are the clear favourites for this New Zealand-based group, but will Italy rise to the occasion or be usurped by one of the southern hemisphere nations?

 **Sweden**

 **South Africa**

Italy

Argentina

MEET THE TEAMS | GROUP H

THE HISTORY OF THE WOMEN'S WORLD CUP

SWEDEN

FIFA WORLD RANKING

3

COLOURS

FIRST — SECOND

NICKNAME: BLÅGULT (BLUE AND YELLOW)

COACH: PETER GERHARDSSON

CAPTAIN: CAROLINE SEGER

BEST WOMEN'S WORLD CUP: RUNNERS-UP (2003)

STAR PLAYER: FRIDOLINA ROLFÖ

A full-back for Barcelona, a rampaging midfielder for her country, Sweden's Footballer of the Year seems capable of shining in any position. In a team sometimes lacking in creativity, Rolfö can provide the spark and chip in with crucial goals.

So near and yet so far is the lament of the Swedish women's team in the big tournaments. In the 2019 Women's World Cup semi-finals they fell to an extra-time goal from the Netherlands; in the 2021 Olympic Games they suffered a heart-breaking loss on penalties in the final against Canada; and in EURO 2022 they met a rampant England in the final four.

Unbeaten in qualification, Sweden enter the 2023 Women's World Cup finals with cautious optimism. Key to coach Gerhardsson's tactics is a strong defence in the hands of the centre-back pairing of Chelsea captain Magdalena Eriksson and PSG's Amanda Ilestedt, along with full-backs Hanna Glas of Bayern Munich and Jonna Andersson, a three-times WSL winner with Chelsea. Each of them has more than 50 caps.

Sweden's attacking play is based on winning back possession and swift counterattacks. Central to this are hard-tackling captain Caroline Seger, Real Madrid playmaker Kosovare Asllani, rising star Johanna Rytting Kaneryd of Chelsea on the right and Barcelona's Fridolina Rolfö wide on the left. Up front, Arsenal's Stina Blackstenius is a battling centre-forward with a sharp goalscoring instinct.

Sweden should progress from a relatively easy group, but their subsequent path to the final is not so favourable. Many will be willing them to finally take their chance, if only for legends like Seger and Asllani who probably won't get another opportunity.

Sweden's captain, Caroline Seger (17) has made over 230 appearances for her country.

GROUP G | SWEDEN AND SOUTH AFRICA

SOUTH AFRICA

FIFA WORLD RANKING

54

COLOURS

FIRST | SECOND

NICKNAME: BANYANA BANYANA
COACH: DESIREE ELLIS
CAPTAIN: JANINE VAN WYK
BEST WOMEN'S WORLD CUP: GROUP STAGE (2019)

South Africa qualified for their second successive Women's World Cup finals by making the semi-finals of WAFCON (Women's Africa Cup of Nations) in July 2022. It was no mean feat, having beaten both Nigeria and Tunisia en route, but they didn't stop there. They beat Zambia with a stoppage time penalty in the semi-final and then lifted the trophy for the first time ever after a 2-1 victory over hosts Morocco.

Coach Desiree Ellis, who scored a hat-trick in Banyana Banyana's first ever match, has been African Coach of the Year for the last three years. Her team ranks among the continent's best and the top players have experience in major leagues. Midfielder Refiloe Jane was the first, going on to star for Canberra United in Australia, then for AC Milan. She was followed by winger Linda Motlhalo, the 'Randfontein Ronaldinho', who spent three years at Swedish club Djurgardens IF. Forward Jermaine Seoposenwe played at Braga and Real Betis, and is now at Mexican club Juárez, and striker Thembi Kgatlana starred for Atlético Madrid before joining Racing Louisville in 2022.

It has to be acknowledged that there is still a significant gap between African nations and most teams at the World Cup, and South Africa lost all their matches at the 2019 Women's World Cup. Recent heavy friendly defeats to Brazil and Australia suggest that unless the spirit of that WAFCON triumph lifts them, they may find 2023 an equally difficult struggle.

ONE TO WATCH: THEMBI KGATLANA

Another star hoping to recover from injury in time for the Women's World Cup, this talented striker was the 2018 African Women's Footballer of the Year. Thembi Kgatlana loves to take defenders on, has netted regularly at the top level in China and Spain, and scored Banyana Banyana's only World Cup goal – so far.

South Africa hope a successful tournament will boost their bid to host the 2027 World Cup finals.

THE HISTORY OF THE WOMEN'S WORLD CUP

ITALY

FIFA WORLD RANKING

16

COLOURS

FIRST | SECOND

NICKNAME: LE AZZURRE

COACH: MILENA BERTOLINI

CAPTAIN: SARA GAMA

BEST WOMEN'S WORLD CUP: QUARTER-FINALS (1999, 2019)

▶ Roma captain and right-back Elisa Bartoli's composure on the ball and pace going forward have won her a regular place in the national team.

For a nation in the vanguard of women's international football in the 1970s and '80s, Italy have consistently underachieved: their greatest achievement is still reaching the Euros final twice in the 1990s. Now Italy find themselves in successive Women's World Cup finals for the first time ever. In 2019 they were the surprise package, beating Brazil and Australia en route to the quarter-finals, and the 2023 squad retains the core of that team, but with some additional and impressive youngsters.

Milena Bertolini likes to set her team out in a solid 4–3–3 formation. A defence built around Italy's 2022 Footballer of the Year, Juventus' Lisa Boattin, Roma's Elisa Bartoli and Sara Gama and AC Milan captain Valentina Bergamaschi rarely concede more than a single goal. Aurora Galli (now at Everton, a rare exception in a squad of home-based players) and Roma's Manuela Giugliano can play as deep-lying midfielders alongside the attacking Arianna Caruso, only 23 and improving every season. Roma's tireless pass-and-move midfielder Giada Greggi, also 23, is staking her place as a regular in the famous blue shirt with a forward line led by Cristiana Girelli, the team's outstanding talent, and her Juventus partner in goals, Barbara Bonansea.

After a poor showing at EURO 2022, many feel the team lack the overall quality to compete with the elite nations. Their defeats to Engand and Belgium in the Arnold Clark Cup in February confirmed those fears. However, Italy will try to keep their defence solid, and trust the experienced strikers to take their chances in tight games.

ONE TO WATCH: CRISTIANA GIRELLI

The winner of the Serie A Best Player award in both 2020 and 2021, Girelli is the focus of Italy's attacking play. The Juventus hotshot scored three goals in the 2019 Women's World Cup and will be looking to net her 50th international goal at the 2023 finals.

GROUP G | ITALY AND ARGENTINA

ARGENTINA

FIFA WORLD RANKING

28

COLOURS

FIRST   SECOND

NICKNAME: LA ALBICELESTE (WHITE AND SKY-BLUES)

COACH: GERMÁN PORTANOVA

CAPTAIN: VANINA CORREA

BEST WOMEN'S WORLD CUP: GROUP STAGE (2003, 2007, 2019)

A year after Argentina's men celebrated their third FIFA World Cup title, the women's team will endeavour to record their first win in four tournaments. The comparison is startling and indicates just how poorly the women's game in Argentina has been managed. After a long struggle, changes are finally arriving, along with hope that 2023 can be a launching pad for La Albiceleste.

France 2019 was deemed a success for Argentina, but top players subsequently refused to play for Carlos Borrello, who had been the coach for 23 years. Germán Portanova took over in 2021 and with hard-earned backing from the Argentinian FA, team morale revived. Playing an attacking, possession-based game, they qualified for the 2023 tournament by achieving third place at the Copa América.

At the finals, Argentina will look to established players to rise to the occasion. They include goalkeeper Vanina Correa, a centre-back pairing of Agustina Barroso, a key player at Palmeiras in Brazil, and Madrid CFF's Aldana Cometti; along with midfielder Mariana Larroquette, Argentina's leading scorer in the modern era. Young midfielders Daiana Falfán and Dalila Ippolito could shine, but most intriguing is the return from three years of self-exile of both midfield star Florencia Bonsegundo, who has continued to prove her worth with Valencia and Madrid CFF, and forward Estefanía Banini, who is simply the best female Argentinian player of her generation.

The 2023 finals might have come too early for Portanova's rebuilt team, but a rejuvenated squad could secure that elusive win and even spring a surprise or two.

▲ Argentina goalkeeper Vanina Correa (1) will be playing in her fourth Women's World Cup finals, 20 years after her tournament debut.

ONE TO WATCH: ESTEFANÍA BANINI

Now playing for Atlético Madrid, she is the classic Argentinian 'enganche'; an elusive, creative force floating between midfield and attack. Despite the fact that she has been away from La Albiceleste for three years and is now 32, hopefully Banini at her best will be on display in New Zealand and Australia.

THE HISTORY OF THE WOMEN'S WORLD CUP

GROUP H

The finalists of the international tournaments from four continents assemble in Australia in an intriguing group in which all teams will believe they can progress

- 🇩🇪 Germany
- 🇲🇦 Morocco
- 🇨🇴 Colombia
- 🇰🇷 South Korea

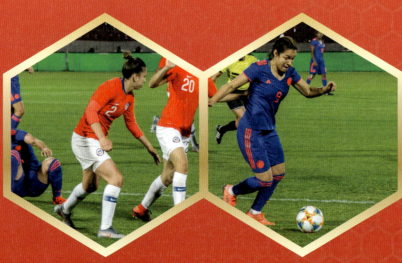

MEET THE TEAMS | GROUP A

THE HISTORY OF THE WOMEN'S WORLD CUP

GERMANY

FIFA WORLD RANKING
2

COLOURS

FIRST — SECOND

NICKNAME: DFB-FRAUENTEAM

COACH: MARTINA VOSS-TECKLENBURG

CAPTAIN: ALEXANDRA POPP

BEST WOMEN'S WORLD CUP: CHAMPIONS (2003, 2007)

For a team who have won the European Championship a record eight times and have been consistently ranked the best or second-best team in the world, Germany's two Women's World Cup triumphs seem a poor return. Despite having failed to make the final in the last three World Cups, expectations – and pressure – will again be high in 2023.

Admittedly they were without competition joint-top scorer Alex Popp, but the narrow extra-time defeat by hosts England in the EURO 2022 final was a bitter disappointment. They quickly recovered though, a 3-0 win over Turkey delivering a Women's World Cup finals place from a tough group that also featured Serbia and Portugal. They travel to Australia with players at the peak of their careers and young stars with tournament experience.

The squad boasts a number of world-class players in goalkeeper Merle Frohms, Wolfsburg defensive partners Marina Hegering and Kathrin Hendrich, driving midfielder Lina Magull, and forwards Lea Schüller and the irrepressible Popp. All are capable of starring at the finals, but so too could the new generation. Among their ranks are magisterial defensive midfielder Lena Oberdorf, voted best young player at EURO 2022; exciting young left-winger Klara Bühl and the 20-year-old attacking midfielder Julie Brand, named as Europe's best young player in 2022.

Germany should manage the group stage fairly easily. They will fear no one, but the knockout stages are likely to throw up some tough challenges, with potential encounters with both France and England before they reach the semi-finals.

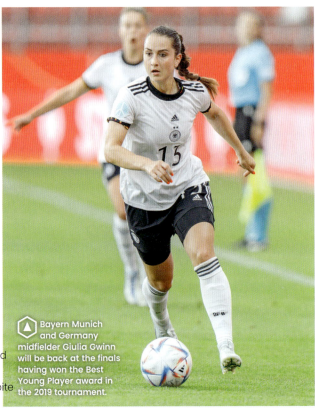

Bayern Munich and Germany midfielder Giulia Gwinn will be back at the finals having won the Best Young Player award in the 2019 tournament.

STAR PLAYER: ALEXANDRA POPP

An instinctive goalscorer, Popp netted in every game she played in at EURO 2022. Strong, powerful and brilliant in the air, it's a good bet that the 32-year-old Wolfsburg striker will add to her tally of three World Cup goals in her third finals.

GROUP H | GERMANY AND MOROCCO

MOROCCO

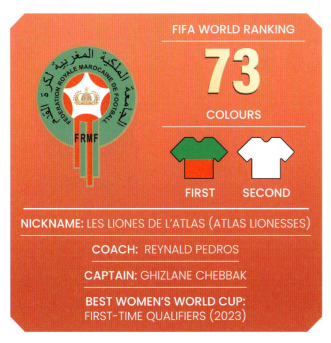

FIFA WORLD RANKING

73

COLOURS

FIRST   SECOND

NICKNAME: LES LIONES DE L'ATLAS (ATLAS LIONESSES)

COACH: REYNALD PEDROS

CAPTAIN: GHIZLANE CHEBBAK

BEST WOMEN'S WORLD CUP: FIRST-TIME QUALIFIERS (2023)

In 2020, the Moroccan Football Federation revealed a long-term strategy to boost women's football in the North African country. Hosting the 2022 WAFCON (Women's Africa Cup of Nations) tournament was part of the plan; beating favourites Nigeria to reach the final for the first time was a dream. Despite losing the final, fans heralded their 'Vice Champions of Africa' who, by reaching the semi-final, had also qualified for their first Women's World Cup finals.

French coach Reynald Pedros, a two-time European Women's Champions League winner with Lyon, took over in 2020. He has shaped the team into a cohesive unit; defensively solid, but they attack with flair and pace. His squad is drawn largely from AS FAR, the dominant club side in Morocco and 2022 African Champions League winners, with international players from the Moroccan diaspora.

The nation's best-known player is striker Ghizlane Chebbak, a prolific goalscorer and inspirational leader, but her young AS FAR teammates, striker Sanaa Mssoudy and Fatima Tagnaout, a left-winger with great pace and control, are also capable of eye-catching displays. Of those born and playing overseas, Yasmin Mrabet, the Levante centre-back, Élodie Nakkach, the Servette and former Dijon midfielder, and forward Rosella Ayane, the Tottenham Hotspur and former England Under-19 international, have all excelled in top European leagues.

The Atlas Lionesses would have wished for an easier group and they will miss the passionate support they had at WAFCON. Qualification in itself is an achievement, though, and it is wonderful to see a plan come together.

▲ Full-back Hanane Aït Hajin whose pace and composure bring strength to the Moroccan defence.

STAR PLAYER: GHIZLANE CHEBBAK

Daughter of Larbi Chebbak, a superstar of Moroccan football, the 32-year-old is a five-time Moroccan Player of the Year and was player of the tournament at the 2022 WAFCON. She is a complete forward, but watch out especially for her deadly free kicks.

THE HISTORY OF THE WOMEN'S WORLD CUP

 # COLOMBIA

FIFA WORLD RANKING
26

COLOURS
FIRST / SECOND

NICKNAME: LAS CHICAS SUPERPODEROSAS (POWERPUFF GIRLS)

COACH: NELSON ABADÍA

CAPTAIN: DANIELA MONTOYA

BEST WOMEN'S WORLD CUP: ROUND OF 16 (2015)

ONE TO WATCH: LINDA CAICEDO

Just 18 years old, the super-skilful Deportivo Cali forward they call 'La Neymar' has the world at her feet. The player of the tournament at the Copa América and the Colombian League's top scorer in 2022, she is already among the game's best players and is surely going to the very top.

For Las Chicas Superpoderosas, 2022 was a magnificent year. They reached the Under-17 Women's World Cup final in India, beat Germany and reached the quarter-finals in the Under-20 tournament, and the senior side made the finals of the Copa América, winning them a place at the 2023 Women's World Cup and the 2024 Olympic Games. Astoundingly, wondergirl Linda Caicedo, upon whom many Colombian fans' hopes rest, played for all three teams.

Colombia's last World Cup outing in 2015 was particularly memorable for their surprising 2-0 victory over France. Eliminated by USA at the first knockout stage, the young team acquitted themselves well. Those players now form the backbone of the 2023 team and they include goalkeeper Catalina Pérez, captain and midfielder Daniela Montoya, whose thunderous strike was one of the best goals of the 2015 tournament, and Catalina Usme, Colombia's all-time top scorer.

The 2023 squad is mainly comprised of home-based players and those playing in Spain's top division, with full-back Manuela Vanegas, midfielder Leicy Santos and forward Mayra Ramírez all making their mark in Europe. However, talented Spanish-based members of the 2015 team, notably Lady Andrade, Yorelli Rincon and Natalia Gaitan, have recently been overlooked. This has made room for the next generation, of which Linda Caicedo is the star, but it also includes other highly rated forwards from the Under-20 team in Gabriela Rodríguez and Gisela Robledo.

Colombia women's football is on a high and, with a little luck – and a certain 18-year-old weaving some magic – this team are capable of repeating and perhaps bettering the heroics of 2015.

Chile in action against Colombia at the Estadio Nacional in Santiago, Chile.

GROUP H | COLOMBIA AND SOUTH KOREA

SOUTH KOREA

FIFA WORLD RANKING

17

COLOURS

FIRST / SECOND

NICKNAME: TAEGEUK NANGJA (TAEGEUK LADIES)

COACH: COLIN BELL

CAPTAIN: KIM HYE-RI

BEST WOMEN'S WORLD CUP: ROUND OF 16 (2015)

Striker Son Hwa-yeon (17) in action during South Korea's impressive 5-0 defeat of Argentina in the 2019 Cup of Nations.

STAR PLAYER: JI SO-YUN

This midfielder won every domestic honour going in her eight years at Chelsea and is probably the WSL's best ever foreign player. Now 32 years old and playing for Suwon FC, Jo So-yun is still able to change a game with her magical passing ability and she is the nation's record goalscorer.

For more than 20 years South Korea have been ranked by FIFA as the top Asian team, but they have had little to show for that status. Their round of 16 finish in the 2015 Women's World Cup – thanks to a 2-1 victory over Spain – being their one achievement of note in recent years.

English coach Colin Bell took charge of the team after their disappointing 2019 Women's World Cup finals, vowing to create a winning mentality and to allow the players the freedom to express themselves. He leads South Korea to their third consecutive World Cup finals, after they finished runners-up the 2022 Women's Asian Cup. It was their best ever placing and their victory over Australia, along with a subsequent draw in a friendly with Canada, show he has made some headway.

The Taegeuk Ladies look to their European-based stars, including South Korea's captain, midfielder and most-capped player Cho So-hyun of Tottenham Hotspur; reliable scorer Lee Geum-min who plays at Brighton and Hove Albion; and Madrid CFF's defensive midfielder Lee Young. The standout star of the home-based contingent is Ji So-Yun, who returned home last season after a stellar career at Chelsea, but the coach will also rely on Incheon Hyundai Steel defender Jang Sel-gi and her teammate, Kang Chae-rim, who has a keen eye for goal.

South Korea's recent form has not been encouraging with a 4-0 thrashing by England and defeats to Italy and Belgium in the 2023 Arnold Cup Cup. If the FIFA rankings are reflected, South Korea should be able to achieve second place in the group, but they will need a winning mentality – and more – if they are to progress in the tournament.

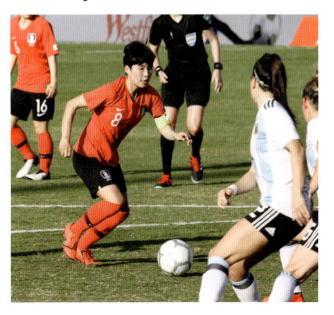

THE HISTORY OF THE WOMEN'S WORLD CUP

THE HISTORY OF THE WOMEN'S WORLD CUP

Unofficial global tournaments had been held in the early 1970s and a number of Mundialitos or 'Little World Cups', were staged in Italy throughout the 1980s (won three times by Italy and twice by England). However, the first FIFA-approved world championship did not take place until 1991. Since then they have been held every four years: a running total of eight Women's World Cup tournaments, each of them with their own drama, spectacle, stars and stories.

THE HISTORY OF THE WOMEN'S WORLD CUP

THE HISTORY OF THE WOMEN'S WORLD CUP

WOMEN'S WORLD CUP CHINA 1991

The first recorded women's international football match took place in 1881, when England met Scotland at Easter Road Stadium in Edinburgh. No one knows who won, because no one kept a note of the score, but it's said that in order to maintain strict Victorian standards of decorum, the players had to play in corsets and bonnets, which must have been quite a sight.

Fast-forward over a century and China was about to host the first ever Women's World Cup or, to give it its official title, the FIFA World Championship for Women's Football for the M&Ms Cup. Of course, there had been women's international tournaments in the intervening decades, not least three years previously, when 12 nations had met, also in China, for what was effectively a trial run for the World Cup (Norway were the winners on that occasion). However, 1991 was the first official Women's World Cup event and it really raised the profile of the women's game around the globe.

The matches were played in stadiums in the southern Chinese province of Guangdong – in its capital, Guangzhou, and the cities of Foshan, Jiangmen, Panyu and Zhongshan – and, as you would expect, there was an official logo and mascot. The latter, which was called Ling Ling, had the head of a Disney-style bird, the body of a human footballer, carried a ball under one arm and brandished a bunch of flowers in the other hand. However, at this tournament the games lasted 80 minutes, rather than the usual 90, and teams were awarded two points for a win rather than the more usual three.

WWC CHINA 1991

THE HISTORY OF THE WOMEN'S WORLD CUP

GROUP STAGE

Group results

Group A	W	D	L	+	–	Pts
China	2	1	0	10	3	5
Norway	2	0	1	6	5	4
Denmark	1	1	1	6	4	3
New Zealand	0	0	3	1	11	0

Group B	W	D	L	+	–	Pts
USA	3	0	0	11	2	6
Sweden	2	0	1	12	3	4
Brazil	1	0	2	1	7	2
Japan	0	0	3	0	12	0

Group C	W	D	L	+	–	Pts
Germany	3	0	0	9	0	6
Italy	2	0	1	6	2	4
Chinese Taipei	1	0	2	2	8	2
Nigeria	0	0	3	0	7	0

The Tianhe Stadium in Guangzhou was packed with 65,000 spectators for the spectacular opening ceremony, which featured a phoenix rising from the ashes to symbolise the rebirth of the women's game and, in Chinese culture, good luck. This was followed by the opening match of the tournament – the Group A game of China versus Norway – which was an equally dazzling spectacle, particularly for the home crowd as there were goals from Ma Li, Sun Qingmei and a brace from Liu Ailing, and the home team won 4-0. This was quite an upset, as Norway were one of the strongest teams in the competition, having appeared in four major finals in the previous four years. China also beat New Zealand, 4-1, and drew 1-1 with Denmark, so they topped the group with five points. All but the bottom team in this group ended up going through to the next stage, so Norway and Denmark progressed along with China, and New Zealand were eliminated, having lost all three of their games.

In Group B, USA made advancing to the next round look easy. Its forward line of captain April Heinrichs, Michelle Akers-Stahl and Carin Jennings, collectively known as the 'Triple-edged Sword', cut a swathe through the opposition and USA finished on six points, having beaten Brazil 5-0 and Japan 3-0. Individually the Brazilians looked good, but the team had only been re-established six months earlier, plus they were missing their playmaker Sissi, whose club hadn't released her. Consequently, they struggled to make an impact, although they did beat Japan 1-0. The Japanese didn't manage a single win and indeed lost humiliatingly to Sweden 8-0. The Swedes secured second place in the group pretty comfortably, only losing to USA, 2-3, although that match was notable for a stunning long-range goal scored by Swedish sub Ingrid Johansson. Two teams from this group went on the knockout stage, so sadly the World Cup campaigns of Brazil and Japan were over.

In Group C the Italians opened well by putting five past Chinese Taipei, with captain Caroline Morace achieving the first ever hat-trick of the Women's World Cup. Germany also looked fresh as they scored four against a young Nigerian side – young individually, but also collectively, because the team had only been established in January that year. The Germans then went on to beat Chinese Taipei 3-0 in a game that was notable for the first ever penalty conversion of the Women's World Cup with Bettina Weigmann beating keeper Lin Hui Fang to hit the back of the net. Italy found it somewhat harder to overcome Nigeria, who were heavily focused on defending. The Italians managed it, though, 12 minutes from full-time when they went ahead courtesy of a goal from the determined Morace, known as 'La Tigre', which proved to be the only goal of the game. The group winner, then, would be the victor of Italy versus Germany and that turned out to be the Germans, who triumphed 2-0, so Germany, Italy and Chinese Taipei were all through to the knockout stage and the women from Nigeria were on the next flight home.

FACT FOCUS

The first woman to referee a Women's World Cup match was Brazil's Cláudia Vasconcelos. She took charge of the third-place play-off, while New Zealand's Linda Black and China's Zuo Xiudi ran the line. There were six women officials at the tournament – the others were Mexico's María Herrera García, Sweden's Ingrid Jonsson and Germany's Gertrud Regus – but Vasconcelos was the only one to referee a game.

WWC CHINA 1991 | GROUP AND KNOCKOUT STAGES

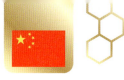

KNOCKOUT STAGE

Knockout results

Quarter-finals
Denmark	1-2	Germany
China	0-1	Sweden
Norway	3-2	Italy
USA	7-0	Chinese Taipei

Semi-finals
Sweden	1-4	Norway
Germany	2-5	USA

Third-place play-off
Sweden	4-0	Germany

▲ Heidi Mohr in action against Nigeria in the group stage. Goals in the quarter-finals and semi-finals would take her 1991 tournament tally to five.

The first quarter-final pitched Denmark against Germany. Each was awarded and converted a penalty – Susan Mackensie scoring for Denmark and Bettina Wiegmann for Germany. However, neither team could break the deadlock and it went to extra-time, the first Women's World Cup to do so, with Heidi Mohr finally getting a header in the 98th minute, two minutes away from penalties, to take Germany through. China versus Sweden was equally hard fought. In front of a passionate 55,000-strong crowd, Zhong Hongolian stopped a penalty and Elisabeth Leidinge in the opposing goal made many valiant saves. In the end an early goal from Swedish captain Pia Sundhage was all that stood between the teams – the host side had shown talent and bravery, but China was out.

Norway faced Italy in the third quarter-final and it was another edge-of-your-seat encounter. Twice Norway went ahead and twice Italy drew level, so it went to extra-time. The game was finally settled with a 96th minute penalty from Norwegian defender Tina Svensson and it ended 3-2 to Norway. The last quarter-final, in which USA met Chinese Taipei, was not so evenly balanced, but was nonetheless remarkable. The final score was 7-0 to USA, with the American Michelle Akers-Stahl becoming the first player to score five times in any Women's World Cup game.

And so to an all-Scandinavian semi-final in which Sweden took on Norway at the Yingdong Stadium in Panyu. Lene Videkull opened the scoring for Sweden in the sixth minute and the Swedes led 1-0 until the 39th minute, when they gave away a penalty. This was neatly dispatched by Tina Svensson, so it was 1-1 going into the break, but Norway renewed their focus and straight after play started again Linda Medalen scored. Her colleague Agnete Carlsen followed suit 25 minutes later and Medalen got a second just before full-time. It was an emphatic 4-1 win for Norway.

At the other semi-final, in Guangzhou's Guangdong Provincial People's Stadium, Germany met USA. German striker Heidi Mohr was in good form and she bagged a first-half goal, with netting in the second half. However, they were missing captain Silvia Neid due to injury and their quarter-final against Denmark had gone to extra-time, so they weren't quite as fresh as the Americans. Ultimately USA's April Heinrichs got two and her teammate Carin Jennings got three. The scoreline was 5-2 and USA were worthy winners in front of a crowd of 15,000 people, which included the footballing legend Pelé.

Determined to come away from the 1991 Women's World Cup with something to show for their efforts, Sweden put everything into the third-place play-off, also at the Guangdong Provincial People's Stadium in Guangzhou. Germany's Marion Isbert was one of the best keepers in the tournament, but she was beaten four times and it ended 4-0, with Sweden, the only team in the tournament to be managed by a woman, Gunilla Paijkull, emerging victorious.

11

THE HISTORY OF THE WOMEN'S WORLD CUP

Germany's Bettina Wiegmann tackles Sweden's Lena Videkoll's during the 1991 3rd place match.

THE HISTORY OF THE WOMEN'S WORLD CUP

1991 FINAL

 NORWAY   1-2   USA

The best teams in a tournament don't always make it through to the final, but at the 1991 Women's World Cup the best teams probably were the finalists Norway, coached by Even Pellerud, and USA, coached by Anson Dorrance – and both teams ardently believed they could win. Norwegian midfielder Hege Riise, who had a 15-year international career and would later go on to coach her national team, said, "When we stood there ready for the final, thinking about everything we had accomplished, we felt confident that we could perform."

There were 63,000 people inside the Tianhe Stadium in Guangzhou and, although it was against the run of play, the first goal came from USA when, after 20 minutes, Michelle Akers-Stahl powered a header at close quarters past Norwegian goalie Reidun Seth, who had passed a late fitness test. However, Norway quickly countered and at 29 minutes Linda Medalen got on the end of a free kick and beat USA keeper Mary Harvey by heading backwards into the net. As they went in at half-time it was 1-1 and it remained that way for much of the second half until, on 78 minutes and with the prospect of extra-time becoming ever more real, Akers-Stahl picked up a hurried back pass from the usually reliable Tina Svensson. The USA striker used her left foot to push the ball out of Seth's reach and her right to slot it home. It was the Americans' 25th goal of the competition and the final result was 2-1 to USA.

The tournament was a high-scoring one with 99 goals scored across 26 matches. Having a total of ten goals to her name, Akers-Stahl received the golden boot. The silver boot went to Germany's Heidi Mohr on seven and USA's Carin Jennings and Norway's Linda Medalen shared the bronze boot with six each. The golden ball for the best performance went to Jennings again, with Akers-Stahl and Medalen the runners-up. There were 32 yellow cards issued and the dubious honour of being the first player to be given a red card in the Women's World Cup went to the Chinese Taipei keeper Lin Hui Fang for a professional foul in the game against Nigeria.

Of course, the first Women's World Cup inevitably produced

Tianhe Stadium in Guangzhou, China, the venue for the first ever Womens' World Cup Final.

a number of firsts, but April Heinrichs had the honour of being the first captain to raise the Women's World Cup trophy, after it had been awarded by FIFA president Joao Havelange. She was also honoured when, on their return home, President George Bush invited the players and coach Dorrance to a reception at the White House in Washington DC, indicating that the tournament had broken through into the public consciousness. In a distinguished international career, Heinrichs was capped 46 times, scored 35 goals and went on to coach the USA national team in 2002 to 2004.

This first iteration of the Women's World Cup, which had seen some great football, some hard-fought contests and some enthusiastic crowds, was unanimously considered a resounding success and an excellent base to build on for the future.

MAGIC MOMENT

Amazingly, Norwegian defender Gunn Nyborg's had played in every single one of Norway's games since the team had been founded and this game was her 100th cap. To mark this impressive achievement she was presented with the match ball by none other than Pelé himself, who was a guest of honour at the event.

WWC CHINA 1991 | FINAL

Two-goal hero, Michelle Akers-Stahl (centre) and teammates Julie Foudy (11) and Carin Jennings (12) celebrate USA's victory in the first ever Women's World Cup final.

THE HISTORY OF THE WOMEN'S WORLD CUP

WOMEN'S WORLD CUP SWEDEN 1995

The 1995 Women's World Cup moved from Asia to Europe, more specifically Sweden. The official mascot, Fiffi, a Humpty Dumpty-shaped character with Viking horns, was yellow and blue, the colours of the Swedish flag, and games were played in stadiums in the capital Stockholm plus four regional cities – Gävle, Helsingborg, Karlstad and Västerås. Some of those venues were the same ones used in 1958, when the men's World Cup had been held in Sweden, and indeed Sweden was the first country to host both men's and women's editions of the tournament.

In parallel with men's football, matches now lasted 90 minutes, rather than the 80 minutes played in China, and teams were awarded three points for a win, rather than two. Again, there were three groups of four countries and nine of those 12 were the same nations that had taken part last time. However, out were Italy, New Zealand and Chinese Taipei, and in were England, Australia and Canada (the latter were included because CONCACAF, the governing body for football in North and Central America and the Caribbean, were given an extra place at the expense of Asia).

The top two in each group, along with the two best third-placed teams, would go through to the quarter-final and semi-final knockout rounds. If a game was tied in normal time there would be extra-time, but in a first for any international competition, a 'golden goal' rule was introduced, so the team who scored first in extra-time would win. The stage was set for a series of exciting encounters.

WWC SWEDEN 1995

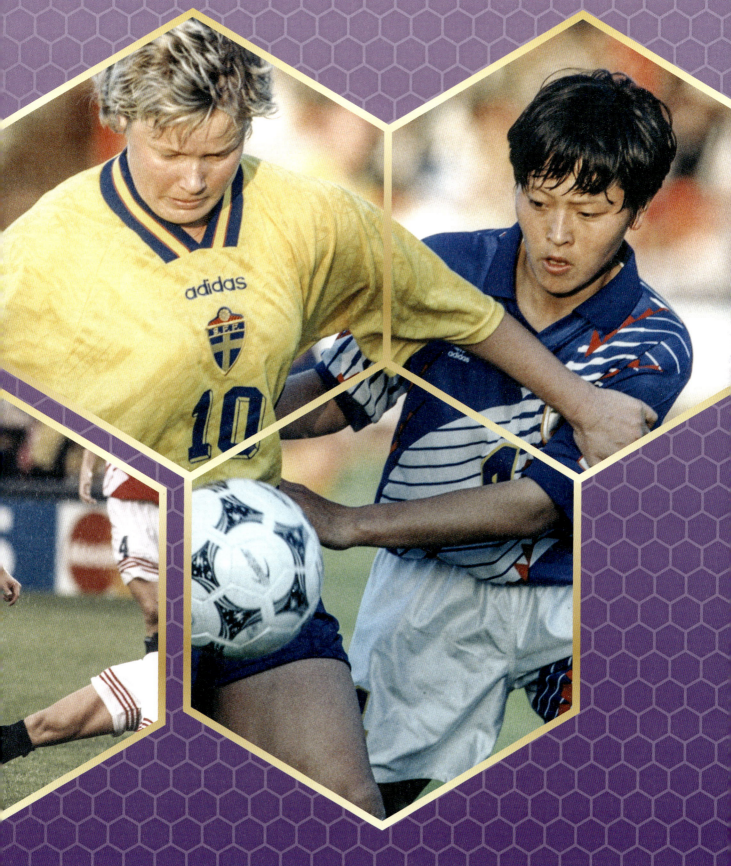

THE HISTORY OF THE WOMEN'S WORLD CUP

GROUP STAGE

Group results

Group A	W	D	L	+	−	Pts
Germany	2	0	1	9	4	6
Sweden	2	0	1	5	3	6
Japan	1	0	2	2	4	3
Brazil	1	0	2	3	8	3

Group B	W	D	L	+	−	Pts
Norway	3	0	0	17	0	9
England	2	0	1	6	6	6
Canada	0	1	2	5	13	1
Nigeria	0	1	2	5	14	1

Group C	W	D	L	+	−	Pts
USA	2	1	0	9	4	7
China	2	1	0	10	6	7
Denmark	1	0	2	6	5	3
Australia	0	0	3	3	13	0

Hosts Sweden were drawn in Group A along with Germany, Japan and Brazil, who they met first. Sweden were expected to dispense with Brazil easily, but the South Americans had other ideas and bested the Scandinavians 1-0. In their next match the Swedes trailed 2-0 to Germany and their prospects didn't look good until Pia Sundhage finally pulled one back and the much-capped Malin Andersson netted another two, so it finished 3-2 to Sweden. After one upset and another near-upset, Sweden's final group game was a straightforward 2-0 win over Japan. The Germans also beat the Japanese, 1-0, and topped the group, due to their 6-1 triumph against the Brazilians, with Sweden second and Japan going through to the next round in third place.

Group B saw another set of comprehensive victories with Norway beating Nigeria 8-0 and Canada 7-0. The Norwegians were also the winners when they met England, but the 2-0 scoreline was rather more respectable, at least from England's point of view. The Norwegians were the clear group winners with nine points and an impressive total of 17 goals and three clean sheets from the three group games, England had acquired six points and was the second team that went through from this group.

Now coached by Tony DiCicco with former captain April Heinrichs as his assistant, former Women's World Cup winners USA were expected to dominate Group C and they won two of their games pretty comfortably, beating Denmark 2-0 (although Mia Hamm had to go in goal when goalkeeper Briana Scurry was sent off) and World Cup debutants Australia 4-1. China, proved to be tougher opposition for them. Tisha Venturini scored first for USA, followed shortly afterwards by teammate Tiffeny Milbrett, but China retaliated before half-time through Wang Liping. Michelle Akers (she had now dropped Stahl from her second name) was still a key USA player and it was a blow when she went off injured, but when play resumed Mia Hamm scored and the Americans led 3-1. USA looked to have the game sewn up until Chinese substitute Wei Haiying pulled one back in the 74th minute and then, in the 79th minute, the great Sun Wen hit an equaliser and it ended in a 3-3 draw.

China had also won their matches against Denmark, 3-1, and Australia, 4-2, so like USA they ended the group stage with seven points. USA topped the table due to a very slightly better goal difference, but both teams were through to the next round and the knockout games, as were Denmark, thanks to the Danes' decisive but solitary victory, 5-0, over the Australians.

Sweden's Anneli Andelén (10) tussles with Japan's Maki Haneta in the Women's World Cup hosts' 2-0 Group A victory.

WWC SWEDEN 1995 | GROUP AND KNOCKOUT STAGES

KNOCKOUT STAGE

Knockout results

Quarter-finals

Germany	3-0	England
(on penalties) China	4-3	Sweden
USA	4-0	Japan
Norway	3-1	Denmark

Semi-finals

Norway	1-0	USA
Germany	1-0	China

Third-place play-off

USA	2-0	China

In the first quarter-final, in Västerås, an England team happy to have made it to the knockout stage were easily dispensed with by Germany 3-0, with goals from Martina Voss, Maren Meinert and Heidi Mohr. The second quarter-final, in Helsingborg, featured host nation, Sweden, and the previous host nation, China. Of course, these two had faced each other at this stage in the last tournament, when Sweden had emerged the victor. On this occasion, China took the lead with a 29th-minute header from Sun Qingmei and held on to that lead all the way through an exciting second half packed with chances for both sides – until Sweden's Ulrika Kalte picked up Malin Andersson's cross and scored with literally just seconds to go. After 90 minutes of normal time it was 1-1 and when extra-time failed to deliver a decisive scoreline, perhaps due to fear of the golden goal, the Women's World Cup produced its first penalty shoot-out, in which China's Gao Hong heroically saved two penalties to take her country through, 4-3.

For the third quarter-final Japan were up against USA in Gävle. Granted, it was a USA team minus Michelle Akers. She was still recovering from a knee injury and that, along with their 16-year-old prodigy Homare Sawa, gave the Japanese a glimmer of hope. However, being without their star striker didn't hold back the reigning champions and with two goals from Kristine Lilly and one apiece from Tiffeny Milbrett and they won 4-0. That left Norway and Denmark to contest the last quarter-final. The Danes were significantly improved since 1991, but were still the underdogs and only managed to put a single consolation goal past ace Norwegian keeper Bente Nordby. It came from substitute Gitte Krogh in the 86th minute, while Gro Espeseth, Linda Medalen and Hege Riise all scored for Norway. The final result in Karlstad was 3-1.

The Arosvallen Stadium in Västerås was the semi-final venue for Norway versus USA and the mighty Michelle Akers had returned from injury, Norway's Ann Kristin Aarønes, who was having an excellent tournament, scored the only goal of the game after just 10 minutes. The Norwegians could have wavered when midfielder Heidi Støre, their most capped player, was sent off in the 76th minute, but they held strong and it ended 1-0 to Norway. The match between Germany and China was a close one, with the two teams only separated by a goal just 11 minutes from the end from Bettina Wiegmann, who capitalised on a poor clearance and put one past Gao Hong in the Chinese goal, meaning in Helsingborg it also finished 1-0, to Germany.

It had been a 3-3 draw when they met earlier in the tournament, so what would the outcome be when China and USA assembled again on the pitch at Strömvallen Stadium in Gävle for the third-place play-off? The only goal of the first half was scored by the on-form Tisha Venturini for USA, but the Americans headed for the dressing room relieved that keeper Briana Scurry had managed to fend off assaults on her goal from China's Sun Wen and Shi Guihong. However, in the 55th minute Mia Hamm sealed the deal 2-0 for USA.

Norway defender Tina Svensson (2) slides in on USA's Mia Hamm (9) in their semi-final in Vasteras, Sweden.

THE HISTORY OF THE WOMEN'S WORLD CUP

Norway's captain Gro Espeseth thwarts Germany's Bettina Wiegmann in the Women's World Cup final in Solna, Sweden.

WWC SWEDEN 1995 | FINAL

1995 FINAL

NORWAY 2-0 GERMANY

▲ The Råsunda Stadium in Stockholm became the first stadium to host the men's and women's final, having staged the mens final in 1958.

And so to the final. Two of the top teams in Europe met at the Råsunda Stadium in Stockholm in from of a crowd of 15,000 people, with many Swedes supporting their close neighbours the Danes. Germany, coached by Gero Bisanz, had beaten their opponents in two recent European Championship finals. Norway, still coached by Even Pellerud, were unbeaten in the competition, but were the losing finalists from four years ago and certainly had something to prove. Both teams were blessed with more than their fair share of talent, but while the Germans' style of play was rather measured and traditional, the Norwegians, led out by Gro Espeseth in place of the suspended Heidi Støre, employed more modern 'press and switch' tactics and were, it's fair to say, the favourites. It was raining heavily and conditions were poor, but after a steady start for both teams Hege Riise hit a special solo goal to put Norway 1-0 up. That strike was in the 37th minute and three minutes later her teammate Marianne Pettersen made it 2-0 to Norway.

Although she was substituted at half-time for the more mature Patricia Brocker, Germany's Birgit Prinz was just 17 when she played in this final and is the youngest player to appear in a World Cup final (Pelé was also 17 when he played in his first final, but Prinz was still younger). However, Germany also had experience in its side, particularly with Heidi Mohr and captain Silvia Neid (who had sat out most of the previous tournament due to injury) firing on all cylinders, but despite throwing everything they had at the Norwegian goal, it wasn't to be. The Norwegians were victorious and could perform the 'snake', the celebration dance they'd devised for the occasion.

In its first European iteration the Women's World Cup had again raised the profile of women's football. Sweden had been excellent hosts plus the home country had won the Fair Play Award. At the end of the tournament, Norwegian Hege Riise was given the golden ball and her teammates Gro Espeseth and Ann Kristin Aarønes received the silver and bronze balls respectively, while in the golden boot competition it was Aarønes who won the golden boot and Riise who took silver. However, it wasn't a completely clean sweep for Norway as the bronze boot went to China's Shi Guihong.

The 1995 Women's World Cup also served as a qualifier for the Olympic Games, which were to be held in the United States, in Atlanta, Georgia, in 1996, and which would feature women's football for the first time (men's football had been a recognised Olympic sport since 1908). FIFA had not had sufficient time to organise a qualifying competition, so it had been decided that the top eight teams from the Women's World Cup would automatically go on to the Olympics the following year. That meant Brazil, China, Denmark, Germany, Japan, Norway, Sweden and USA would soon meet again.

MAGIC MOMENT

Speaking many years later, Norway's Hege Riise said, 'Some moments you just can't forget and that goal in the final is one for me.' She added, 'Although we were so clearly on top, we always knew it was Germany, who never give up, so we didn't relax until the final whistle. Then we really had a party.'

THE HISTORY OF THE WOMEN'S WORLD CUP

▶ Norway's goalkeeper Bente Nordby is surrounded by jubilant teammates as she raises the Women's World Cup trophy aloft in the Råsunda Stadium.

THE HISTORY OF THE WOMEN'S WORLD CUP

WOMEN'S WORLD CUP USA 1999

This is generally considered to be the landmark Women's World Cup tournament; the one that truly forced its way into the public's consciousness and insisted that women's football be taken seriously. The 1999 edition was held in USA and people flocked to the games, with the final taking place in front of more than 90,000 spectators at the Rose Bowl in Pasadena, California. Attendance records were broken at every stage of the competition – the average gate was almost 38,000. However, all the matches were also broadcast live around the world and that was crucial in opening up the sport to an even wider audience and enabling it to break through to the mainstream.

More people were watching, but there was also more to watch, as the number of national sides challenging for the trophy increased by four to 16. The teams were divided up into four groups of four with the top two progressing to the next stage and games were played at eight venues right across the USA. As well as Pasadena, in the west stadiums in San Francisco, San José and Portland were used; in the east the stadiums were in Boston, New Jersey and Washington DC, plus Chicago.

The mascot was a smiley fox called Nutmeg and, for the first time, all the referees and match officials were women. Such was the enthusiasm for the game, that following the tournament a USA Women's United Soccer Association was set up (although it collapsed after three seasons due to financial problems) and many players, particularly those playing for the host nation, ended the tournament as household names – Brandi Chastain being the most obvious one.

WWC USA 1999

THE HISTORY OF THE WOMEN'S WORLD CUP

GROUP STAGE

Group results

Group A	W	D	L	+	−	Pts
USA	3	0	0	13	1	9
Nigeria	2	0	1	5	8	6
North Korea	1	0	2	2	4	6
Denmark	0	0	03	1	8	0

Group B	W	D	L	+	−	Pts
Brazil	2	1	0	12	4	7
Germany	1	2	0	10	4	5
Italy	1	1	1	3	3	4
Mexico	0	0	3	1	15	0

Group C	W	D	L	+	−	Pts
Norway	3	0	0	13	2	9
Russia	2	0	1	10	3	6
Canada	0	1	2	3	12	1
Japan	0	1	2	1	10	1

Group D	W	D	L	+	−	Pts
China	3	0	0	12	2	9
Sweden	2	0	1	6	3	6
Australia	0	1	2	3	7	1
Ghana	0	1	2	1	10	1

Boy band NSYNC and girl group B*Witched had entertained the crowd at the opening ceremony and after just 17 minutes Mia Hamm opened the scoring for the home nation against Denmark. The Group A game ended 3-0, with additional goals from Julie Foudy and native New Yorker Kristine Lilly. However, in USA's second match, against Nigeria, it looked like an upset could be on the cards. Nigerian Nkiru Okosieme scored after just 73 seconds, but USA retaliated swiftly and it was 6-1 at half-time, although the second half was quieter and it finished 7-1. USA topped the group and Nigeria, having won their other two games, against Denmark and North Korea, achieved second place.

The story in Group B, the group of death, wasn't quite so clear cut, although when much improved Brazil played Women's World Cup debutants Mexico the scoreline echoed that of the USA–Nigeria game – 7-1 to Brazil with Pretinha and Sissi both scoring hat-tricks, and Kátia getting the other one.

Germany put six past Mexico to no reply, but managed a 1-1 draw with Italy and then a hard-fought 3-3 draw with Brazil. In the bottom-of-the-table battle Italy bested Mexico 2-0, so Brazil and Germany progressed to the knockout stage.

There was another 7-1 scoreline in Group C, when defending champions Norway thrashed Canada. Wins against Russia and Japan cemented Norway's position at the top of the table and thus qualification for the next round. Newbies Russia went through with them, thanks to decisive wins against Japan, 5-0, and Canada, 4-1. Hooper scored again for the Canadians, but across these two matches Russia's goalscoring honours were shared among seven players, including forward Natalia Barbashina and captain Irina Grigorieva, and the Russian team looked balanced and strong.

The opening game in Group D saw old foes China and Sweden pitted against each other. Sweden's Kristin Bengtsson wasted no time, scoring in the second minute, but Jin Yan equalised 15 minutes later. The decider came from China's Liu Ailing halfway through the second half. The Chinese put seven past Ghana, with Sun Wen netting a hat-trick, and three past Australia, with Sun Wen getting two, although Cheryl Salisbury did pull one back and salvaged some pride for the Australians. Sweden won both their other games, 2-0 against Ghana and 3-1 against Australia, while Ghana and Australia drew 1-1, so it was China and Sweden who moved on to the quarter-finals.

▲ Pretinha hit a hat-trick for Brazil against Mexico in the group stage, but couldn't help her team overcome Nigeria in the quarter-final.

WWC USA 1999 | GROUP AND KNOCKOUT STAGES

KNOCKOUT STAGE

Knockout results

Quarter-finals
China	2-0	Russia
Norway	3-1	Sweden
USA	3-2	Germany
(after extra-time) Brazil	4-3	Nigeria

Semi-finals
China	5-0	Norway
USA	2-0	Brazil

Third-place play-off
(on penalties) Brazil	5-4	Norway

Sun Wen of China (L) and Norway's Goril Kringen fight for the ball in their semi-final game at Foxboro Stadium, Massachusetts.

In the first quarter-final, at the Spartan Stadium in San José, China attacked Russia mercilessly, but Russian goalkeeper Svetlana Petko kept her cool admirably until the 37th minute, when 18-year-old Pu Wei hit a long-range shot that slipped under Petko and across the line. The Chinese then made it two in the 56th minute when a Sun Wen free kick bounced off the post and was poked home by Jin Yan. Goodbye Russia. Later that day in the same stadium it was an all-Scandi affair as Sweden faced Norway. A Swedish team in the process of being rebuilt looked lively and determined, but it was goalless at half-time. However, in the second half, in the space of 21 minutes, the Norwegian trio of Ann Kristin Aarønes, Marianne Pettersen and Hege Riise all found the back of the net. Sweden responded with a goal in the 91st minute from Malin Moström, but it was too little too late and they were out.

The third quarter-final, at the Jack Kent Cooke Stadium in Washington DC in front of US president Bill Clinton, pitted hosts USA against Germany. The first goal came after five minutes and was scored by USA's Brandi Chastain – for Germany. Fortunately, Tiffeny Milbrett evened it up after 16 minutes, but just before half-time Bettina Wiegmann put Germany ahead again. Chastain herself made amends just after half-time by equalising. It was 2-2 but at 66 minutes Joy Fawcett got a third for USA and it ended 3-2. Also played in Washington DC, the fourth quarter-final was the first to feature an African or South American side, and the first to be decided on a golden goal. At half-time Brazil were leading 3-0, but in the second half Nigeria heroically hit three and drew level, so at full-time it was 3-3 and extra-time beckoned. The winner came from Brazilian star Sissi. When she blasted the ball at the Nigerian goal, it hit the post and ricocheted in. They had acquitted themselves admirably, but it was heartbreak for the Nigerians.

There were no two ways about it: China absolutely smashed it in their semi-final against Norway at Boston's Foxboro Stadium. Skipper Sun Wen was first on the scoresheet in the third minute, followed by Liu Ailing, who found the back of the net with two volleys, either side of half-time. Fan Junjie was next, in the 65th minute and finally Sun Wen again slotted home a penalty in the 72nd minute, all to no reply from Norway. It ended 5-0 to China. In the other semi-final, at a packed Stanford Stadium in San Francisco, USA took on Brazil. The hosts had a lot to thank goalkeeper Briana Scurry for as Sissi and her Brazilian teammates never gave up, but an early goal from Cindy Parlow and a late penalty from Michelle Akers meant that USA won 2-0 and were through to the final.

It was an exciting game, but in essence the story of the third-place play-off was very simple. Both sides had chances, but neither Brazil nor Norway could break through the other team's defence to score at the Rose Bowl in Pasadena, so it went to extra time and then penalties – for the first time in the history of the Women's World Cup – ending in a Brazilian victory and Norwegian disappointment.

THE HISTORY OF THE WOMEN'S WORLD CUP

▲ President Bill Clinton is presented with a jersey by Julie Foudy and other members of the 1999 USA World Cup winning team at a White House reception.

THE HISTORY OF THE WOMEN'S WORLD CUP

1999 FINAL

 USA 5-4 CHINA

(on penalties)

There was a four-jet fly-past, and Jennifer Lopez and Hanson performed for the 90,000-strong crowd. It was a big occasion, a hot day and the atmosphere in the Pasadena Rose Bowl for the USA versus China Women's World Cup final was electric. This is how they lined up.

In an all-white strip and coached by Tony DiCicco, the USA team's 4–3–3 formation consisted of Mia Hamm, Tiffeny Milbrett and Cindy Parlow in the forward line, supported by a midfield of Michelle Akers, flanked by Julie Foudy and Kristine Lilly. In defence, the centre-backs were captain Carla Overbeck and Kate Sobrero, with Joy Fawcett and Brandi Chastain at full-back, and Briana Scurry in goal. China, all in red and coached by Ma Yuanan, played 4–4–2 and had Gao Hong between the sticks, Wen Lirong and Fan Yunjie at centre-back, and Bai Jie and Wang Liping at full-back. The midfield was made up of Zhao Lihong, Liu Ailing, Liu Ying and Pu Wei, with a strike force of Jin Yan and captain Sun Wen.

Both teams were worthy finalists and it was a very evenly matched contest, so after a high-tempo start from the USA the game swiftly settled down, with both sides finding it hard to gain the upper hand. Prior to the third-place play-off, which had been played in the same stadium before the final, there hadn't been a 0-0 draw in 82 World Cup games. However, like the play-off, at the end of normal time the final was scoreless, so the teams played on.

What was probably the most promising opportunity for either side came in extra-time, when China's Fan Yunjie almost headed in that elusive golden goal, only for USA's quick-thinking Kristine Lilly to clear it off the line, but at the end of extra-time it was still scoreless – the crowd that day didn't see a goal in a full four hours of open play – so the Women's World Cup final would be decided on penalties.

China were first up and Xie Huilin, who had come on for Jin Yan, scored, as did Carla Overbeck who took the first penalty for USA. Next was Qiu Haiyan, who had replaced Zhao Lihong, and she hit the back of the net, just like Joy Fawcett. In the third round, Liu Ying stepped up, but USA keeper Briana Scurry saved her shot (although Scurry clearly left her line

▲ The legendary Rose Bowl in Pasadena, California played host to the 1999 final, just five years after it had staged the men's final.

and the penalty should technically have been retaken), so when Kristine Lilly scored, USA had the advantage. The pairing of Zhang Ouying and Mia Hamm both converted, as did Sun Wen, so the pressure was all on Brandi Chastain. She stepped calmly and confidently up, and drove the ball home with her left foot, slotting it past Gao to clinch USA's second Women's World Cup title, this time on their home turf. To say the spectators in the stadium – and no doubt the 17.9 million people glued to their TV sets across USA – went wild would be an understatement!

MAGIC MOMENT

Brandi Chastain dropped to her knees, removed her shirt and raised her fist in celebration. Although she was criticised at the time for being 'unfeminine' and 'inappropriate', this image quickly became iconic, appearing on the cover of multiple newspapers as well as prestigious American magazines like *Time* and *Sports Illustrated*.

WWC USA 1999 | FINAL

Carla Overbeck hods the Women's World Cup trophy aloft after defeatibg China in the final.

THE HISTORY OF THE WOMEN'S WORLD CUP

WOMEN'S WORLD CUP
USA 2003

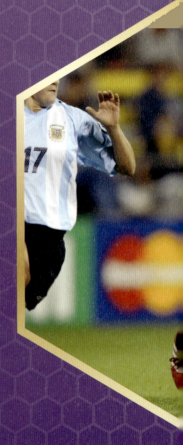

The 2003 Women's World Cup was originally scheduled to take place in China, but in May an outbreak of SARS (a virus similar to COVID-19), caused a last-minute location switch, so come September that year, players, coaches and support staff from 16 countries, including debutants France, Argentina and South Korea, headed for the USA. This was the obvious choice, because the USA had recent experience of hosting major football tournaments plus the infrastructure necessary to stage an event of this size was already in place, but as a consequence of the change there was no mascot for the 2003 event.

China was awarded the next Women's World Cup, scheduled for 2007, and retained its automatic qualification for 2003. This was perhaps fortunate, because the Chinese couldn't necessarily claim to be the best team in Asia, having been beaten by the Democratic People's Republic of Korea (North Korea) in the final of the 2003 AFC Women's Championship in June. Third and four places in that tournament had gone to Republic of Korea (South Korea) and Japan respectively, both of whom were taking part in the World Cup.

The teams were divided into four groups of four, with the winners and runners-up in each group going through to the knockout stage. In total, 32 matches would be played at six venues (from west to east): Home Depot Center in Los Angeles, California; PGE Park in Portland, Oregon; Columbus Crew Stadium in Columbus, Ohio; RFK Memorial Stadium in Washington DC; Lincoln Financial Field in Philadelphia, Pennsylvania; and Gillette Stadium in Boston, Massachusetts.

WWC USA 2003

THE HISTORY OF THE WOMEN'S WORLD CUP

GROUP STAGE

Group results

Group A	W	D	L	+	−	Pts
USA	3	0	0	11	1	9
Sweden	2	0	1	5	3	6
North Korea	1	0	2	3	4	3
Nigeria	0	0	3	0	11	0

Group B	W	D	L	+	−	Pts
Brazil	2	1	0	8	2	7
Norway	2	0	1	10	5	6
France	1	1	1	2	3	4
South Korea	0	0	3	1	11	0

Group C	W	D	L	+	−	Pts
Germany	3	0	0	13	2	9
Canada	2	0	1	7	5	6
Japan	1	0	2	7	6	3
Argentina	0	0	3	1	15	0

Group D	W	D	L	+	−	Pts
China	2	1	0	3	1	7
Russia	2	0	1	5	2	6
Ghana	1	0	2	5	2	3
Australia	0	1	2	3	5	1

The new host nation, whose line-up included the great Mia Hamm, easily topped Group A – the tournament's group of death – scoring nine points and a total of 11 goals. USA conceded just the one, when Sweden's Victoria Svensson bypassed goalkeeper Briana Scurry to hit the back of the net. In the same game, USA legend Brandi Chastain broke her foot and came off having played just 45 minutes. Svensson scored again against the Democratic People's Republic of Korea (North Korea), and against Nigeria her teammate Hanna Ljungberg got two, with captain Malin Moström bagging one. That all meant Sweden came second in the group, with North Korea, who had beaten Nigeria 3-0, third and the Nigerians last.

Things were less clear-cut in Group B. The opening game saw Norway overcome France 2-0. The Norwegians also beat South Korea with the devastating scoreline of 7-1, but they lost to Brazil 4-1. France subsequently bested South Korea and managed a draw with Brazil, Marinette Pichon, 2003's joint top scorer in USA's Women's United Soccer Association (WUSA) (along with Norway's Dagny Mellgren) getting the French equaliser in the 92nd minute. However, in the end it was the Brazilian team, notable for a teenage prodigy called Marta Vieira da Silva – more commonly known as simply Marta – who went straight through with seven points. Norway on six were also through to the next round, with France trailing on four and South Korea failing to get off the mark.

Meanwhile, in Group C Germany were dominant, putting four past Canada (Germany's Bettina Wiegmann also netted her 50th international goal in that match), three past Japan and humiliating Argentina by putting six past them – not the best way to mark the Argentinians first appearance at a Women's World Cup. Unfortunately, they ended the group stage pointless, after losing to both Canada and Japan as well, although the latter match, which ended 6-0 to Japan, did see Japan's Mio Otani produce the only hat-trick of the tournament. It was a good win for Japan, but the Canadians beat them to secure second place, with the Germans comfortably in first.

China and Russia were the heavyweights in Group D, along with Oceania champions Australia and Ghana, who were the lowest-ranked team of the tournament, even though they were the winners of the Women's Africa Cup of Nations in 2002. It was Australia who finished bottom, though – the team managed to gain a point by holding China to a 1-1 draw, but lost 2-1 to both Russia and Ghana. The final placings came down to a tussle between China and Russia in which Russian goalie Alla Volkova heroically kept out successive shots from the Chinese. There was a missed penalty, but a single goal from Bai Jie sealed the deal and China, captained by giant of the game Sun Wen, topped the group, followed by Russia.

FACT FOCUS

In a long international career, Birgit Prinz was capped 214 times and scored 128 goals for Germany. By the time the Women's World Cup 2003 ended, she had picked up both the Golden Ball and Golden Boot trophies, having scored a total of seven goals.

WWC USA 2003 | GROUP AND KNOCKOUT STAGES

KNOCKOUT STAGE

Knockout results

Quarter-finals
Brazil	1-2	Sweden
USA	1-0	Norway
Germany	7-1	Russia
China	0-1	Canada

Semi-finals
USA	0-3	Germany
Sweden	2-1	Canada

Third-place play-off
USA	3-1	Canada

For the first quarter-final, at Boston's Gillette Stadium, a youthful Brazilian side, average age just 22, faced more experienced Sweden. Victoria Svensson opened for the Swedes, but on the cusp of half-time Marta equalised from the penalty spot, after being brought down by goalkeeper Sofia Lundgren. In the 53rd minute Sweden had a free kick 22 metres out, which was converted by Malin Andersson. Sweden had recently struggled to beat Brazil, but on this occasion they held on and the match finished 2-1.

USA's opposition were Norway, who had recalled veterans Marianne Pettersen and Bente Nordby from retirement. This turned out to be a smart move with goalkeeper Nordby proving particularly invaluable – crucially, she parried a 67th-minute Mia Hamm penalty. However, in the 24th minute USA's Abby Wambach had headed what ended up being the game's only goal. The final score in the Gillette Stadium was 1-0 to USA.

Germany had a strong record against Russia, having scored 29 and conceded just two in their last ten meetings, so at half-time when Germany led by a single goal, a 25th-minute Martina Müller strike, Russia were entitled to feel they were doing alright. However, once play resumed at Portland's PGE Park, the Russians, led by 37-year-old Marina Burakova, the tournament's oldest player, couldn't hold on. They let in six more, including two each from Kerstin Garefrekes and Birgit Prinz, but at least 16-year-old Elena Danilova got one back, and it ended 7-1.

PGE Park was the venue again for China versus Canada. China had won ten of their last 12 meetings. Canada, however, had Christine Sinclair, star of the local University of Portland team, playing in her first Women's World Cup, and Christine Latham, WUSA 2003 Rookie of the Year. It was decided by a single goal, from Charmaine Hooper in the seventh minute, and finished 1-0 to Canada.

In the semis, USA met Germany, again in Portland. It was closely fought from the off, but after 15 minutes the ball hit the bar and was headed home by Kerstin Garefrekes. Both goalkeepers, USA's Briana Scurry and Germany's Silke Rottenberg, were kept busy, but USA desperately needed an equaliser. Substitute Tiffeny Milbrett, brought on as a third striker, had a penalty appeal denied and then, as USA continued to push forward, the Germans Maren Meinert and Birgit Prinz both countered and scored, at 91 and 93 minutes respectively. Germany had won 3-0 and the hosts were out.

In the other semi-final, once more in Portland, Canada, coached by Norwegian Even Pellerud, went straight on the attack against Sweden, but the Scandinavians reciprocated in kind, forcing Pellerud to change his formation. It was goalless for over an hour until the 64th minute, when teenager Kara Lang's powerful free kick flew past keeper Caroline Jönsson to give the Canadians the lead. However, Swedish captain Malin Moström equalised in the 79th minute, with Josefine Öqvist scoring to win it for Sweden, 2-1, in the 86th minute.

The stage was set for an all-European final and an all-North American third place play-off at the Home Depot Center in Los Angeles. Christine Sinclair scored for Canada, but USA won 3-1 with goals from Kristine Lilly, Shannon Boxx and Tiffeny Millbrett.

Mia Hamm in action for USA in the third-place play-off against Canada.

THE HISTORY OF THE WOMEN'S WORLD CUP

▶ Japan's Mio Otani evades Argentina defender Valeria Cotelo during Japan's 6-0 victory at Crew Stadium in Columbus, Ohio.

THE HISTORY OF THE WOMEN'S WORLD CUP

German defender Ariane Hingst watches Hanna Lungberg as Sweden attack in the final.

WWC USA 2003 | FINAL

2003 FINAL

 GERMANY 2-1 SWEDEN

▲ The LA Galaxy's Home Depot Center was a 27,000 seater stadium built specifically for soccer. It staged the third-place play-off and the final of the 2003 World Cup.

The final, played in front of 26,000 spectators at LA Galaxy's Home Depot Center stadium, was a repeat of the Women's EURO 2001 final, when Germany beat Sweden by a single goal – a 98th-minute winner scored under the golden goal rule. Having knocked out USA, the hosts and top seeds, Germany went into the final as favourites. They were unbeaten in the tournament and had amassed 15 goals in four matches. But no one was underestimating a Swedish team who had shown incredible resolve to emerge from the 'group of death' and displayed extraordinary semi-final heroics.

Both teams were set out in a 4-4-2 formation with attacking prowess to the fore. Sweden's striking partnership of Hanna Ljungberg and Victoria Svensson had shared five goals in the finals, while Germany fielded Maren Meinert, playing a little deeper than Birgit Prinz, who was now being hailed as the world's best player.

It was Sweden who took control of the match, having most of the possession as Germany looked to counter-attack, with Prinz a constant threat to the Swedish goal. As the half progressed both she and Ljungberg had chances that were thwarted by the respective goalkeepers. There was little Rottenberg could do about Ljungberg's strike in the 41st minute though. Her well-timed run between two defenders was spotted by Svensson, whose pass into space left the striker to slot the ball past the keeper.

Sweden deserved their first-half lead, but retained it for just one minute after the break. Prinz, playing the target striker role to perfection, collected the ball with her back to goal and fed Meinert on the corner of the penalty area. The veteran had time to advance, steady herself and side-foot the ball into the corner of the net.

Now the first-half roles were reversed. Germany were on the front foot with Sweden forced to counter-attack. The chances came thick and fast, mostly for the Germans, as Prinz twice went close, Wunderlich missed an open goal, and Wiegmann and Hingst had efforts denied by Joensson, the Swedish goalkeeper, who made save after save. Then, as the match entered its last ten minutes, Sweden came to life. Svensson and Ljungberg both carved out glorious opportunities that went agonisingly wide.

Extra-time would last only eight minutes, cut short by the sudden death of the golden goal. It came from an unlikely source. Substitute Nia Kuenzer had been sent on to shore up the German defence with just two minutes of normal time left. Now venturing upfield for a free kick, she rose by the penalty spot to meet Lingor's inch-perfect free-kick with a forceful header that gave Joensson no chance. Match over: the brave Swedes sat stunned by the instant defeat, while the Germans celebrated being Champions of the World for the first time ever.

It was a fittingly exciting match for a final. Player of the match and victorious captain Wiegmann was spot on when she said, 'We saw everything that a soccer game needs. There were a lot of chances, toughness, it was close, and well fought, but in the end I think it was a lucky goal for us.'

THE HISTORY OF THE WOMEN'S WORLD CUP

WOMEN'S WORLD CUP CHINA 2007

Four years later than originally anticipated due to the 2003 SARS outbreak, and 16 years after it had hosted the inaugural tournament, China was the location for the 2007 Women's World Cup, and the event was symbolised by the official mascot, a cute little girl with bunches and a football under her arm called Hua Mulan.

However, this time the games were played much further afield and over a much wider area, beyond Guangzhou and Guangdong Province, in Chengdu, Hangzhou, Tianjin and Wuhan, but not in Beijing, which was caught up in preparations for the 2008 Olympic Games. This meant that Shanghai became the venue for the opening ceremony and for the final itself.

Unusually, on this occasion there were no World Cup debutants (the only time that had happened before was at the first competition in 1991). Once more there were four groups of four, with the top two from each group progressing to the quarter-final and then semi-final knockout stages. Group B was the one designated the 'group of death' as it contained three of the top five teams in FIFA's world rankings – USA (first), Sweden (third) and North Korea (fifth).

It's also worth noting that FIFA made a change to the regulations and dispensed with the golden goal rule, which had been introduced at the 1995 tournament, although in the event the possibility of a golden goal didn't arise anyway, as none of the matches went to extra-time (and therefore none went to a penalty shoot-out either).

WWC CHINA 2007

THE HISTORY OF THE WOMEN'S WORLD CUP

GROUP STAGE

Group results

Group A	W	D	L	+	–	Pts
Germany	2	1	0	13	0	7
England	1	2	0	8	3	5
Japan	1	1	1	3	4	4
Argentina	0	0	3	0	18	0

Group B	W	D	L	+	–	Pts
USA	2	1	0	5	2	7
North Korea	1	1	1	5	4	4
Sweden	1	1	1	3	4	4
Nigeria	0	1	2	1	4	1

Group C	W	D	L	+	–	Pts
Norway	2	1	0	10	4	7
Australia	1	2	0	7	4	5
Canada	1	1	1	7	4	4
Ghana	0	0	3	3	15	0

Group D	W	D	L	+	–	Pts
Brazil	3	0	0	10	0	9
China	2	0	1	5	6	6
Denmark	1	0	2	4	4	3
New Zealand	0	0	3	0	9	0

Group B, that so-called 'group of death', certainly was hard fought. Coincidentally, the same four teams – USA, Sweden, North Korea and Nigeria – had all been in the same group at the previous Women's World Cup. USA topped the table on both occasions, but dropped a couple of points this time round after being held to a 2-2 draw by North Korea. As a result of that draw, and the fact that they beat Nigeria 2-0, North Korea ended up on four points, as did Sweden, who lost to USA, drew with Nigeria and beat North Korea. In 2003 Sweden progressed. In 2007 it was North Korea who went through, simply because they had scored one more goal.

The tournament had kicked off with Germany versus Argentina in Group A, a match that ended with a record 11-0 scoreline in Germany's favour and featured three goals apiece from Birgit Prinz and Sandra Smisek, and two goals each from Melanie Behringer and Renate Lingor. England also beat the Argentinians, but 'only' 6-1, although England's Jill Scott scored her first international goal in this game. England were held to a 2-2 draw by Japan, although Kelly Smith scored two superb goals in just three minutes, but managed to hold the Germans to a 0-0 draw, so the stage finished with Germany on seven points and England on five. They both went through, while Japan on four points and Argentina with no points didn't.

There was excitement and tension in Group C, too, as Australia won a Women's World Cup game for the first time, scoring four against Ghana, although teenager Anita Amankwa did pull one back for the Africans. Australia achieved a 2-2 draw against Canada and, perhaps more impressively, a 1-1 draw against Norway, ultimately putting them in second place in the table with five points. When Norway won the Women's World Cup in 1995 they were coached by Even Pellerud and he was back in 2007 as coach of the Canadian team, so the meeting between the two teams was potentially something of a grudge match. Either way, Norway were the victors, 2-1, and, having beaten Ghana 7-2, they topped the group with seven points.

Group D's Brazilian team were the only nation to emerge from the group stage with a maximum nine points. They started by beating New Zealand 5-0, with Marta getting two and Cristiane one. They then – and this was the result that sent shockwaves through the tournament – went on to beat hosts China 4-0, with Marta, and this time Cristiane as well, getting two. China's recently appointed coach, Marika Domanski-Lyfors, who had previously played for and coached the Swedish national side, had targeted a top-four finish for her new charges, so losing to Brazil was a blow. However, China succeeded in beating Denmark 3-2 – this was a closely contested game and China's winner only came in the 88th minute – and New Zealand 2-0, and six points was sufficient to see them through in second place.

FACT FOCUS

China, managed by the Swede Marika Domanski-Lyfors, were knocked out of the Women's World Cup 2007 by a goal from a Norwegian teenager called Isabell Herlovsen. In her previous job, coaching her home country, Domanski-Lyfors' Sweden were knocked out of the EURO 2005 by... a Norwegian teenager called Isabell Herlovsen.

WWC CHINA 2007 | GROUP AND KNOCKOUT STAGES

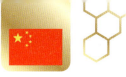

KNOCKOUT STAGE

Knockout results

Quarter-finals
Germany	3-0	North Korea
USA	3-0	England
Norway	1-0	China
Brazil	3-2	Australia

Semi-finals
Germany	3-0	Norway
Brazil	4-0	USA

Third-place play-off
USA	4-1	Norway

North Korea had made it to the knockout stage for the first time in three tournaments, but their quarter-final opposition were Germany, in form and current European and world champions. Captain Ri Kum Suk and Kim Yong Ae attacked Nadine Angerer's goal valiantly, but Kerstin Garefrekes broke through North Korea's defence to score just before half-time. In the 67th minute Renate Lingor got Germany's second and five minutes later German captain Annike Krahn made it 3-0. The North Koreans' adventure was over and the Germans were semi-final-bound.

England also met tough opposition, but it was still 0-0 at half-time in their match versus USA. However, the Americans came out all guns blazing. Abby Wambach's header found the back of the net in the 48th minute; Shannon Boxx hit a low shot past England goalkeeper Rachel Brown in the 57th minute; and USA captain Kristine Lilly, who was 36 and at the time the oldest scorer ever in the Women's World Cup, netted in the 60th minute. It finished 3-0 to USA. Disappointed England were going home, but USA were through.

You had to feel sorry for the Chinese team. They had certainly been revitalised by their first foreign coach, Marika Domanski-Lyfors, who had improved their fitness and motivation. However, they couldn't get the ball past veteran Norwegian keeper Bente Nordby and the only goal was scored by teenager Isabell Herlovsen in the 32nd minute. It was 1-0 to Norway and the hosts were out.

In the fourth quarter-final Formiga unleashed a blistering shot that put Brazil ahead against Australia after just four minutes. Marta added another in the 23rd minute, but the Australians' Lisa De Vanna pulled one back at 36 minutes. The Matildas got another with Lauren Colthorpe's 68th-minute header, but Cristiane's 75th-minute shot meant no fairy-tale ending for Australia. It ended 3-2 to Brazil.

In the first semi-final the two teams were pretty evenly matched until just before half-time an unfortunate own goal from Norway's Tine Rønning put Germany in the lead. The Norwegians worked hard to level the scoreline, but at 72 minutes Kerstin Stegemann's deflected goal made their task a lot harder and three minutes later Martina Müller sealed the deal for the Germans. They would be making another World Cup final appearance.

An own goal got the second semi-final going, too, when Brazil's Formiga took a corner after 20 minutes and USA's Leslie Osborne booted it into her own net. Marta followed up after 27 minutes and, to add to the American's woes, Shannon Boxx was sent off just before half-time. An unmarked Cristiane scored at 56 minutes and Marta got her second at 79 minutes. USA had been well and truly knocked out of the competition, 4-0 to Brazil.

However, USA, keen to regain some pride, dispatched Norway 4-1 in the third-place play-off. This match saw the end of several illustrious Women's World Cup careers, including that of Norway's legendary striker Ragnhild Gulbrandsen, USA's Kristine Lilly, who had played in every single one of her nation's 50 international matches, and both countries' goalkeepers, Bente Nordby and Briana Scurry.

German players, Annike Krahn (5), goalkeeper Nadine Angerer and Sonja Fuss (15) celebrate their emphatic 3-0 semi-final defeat of Norway.

THE HISTORY OF THE WOMEN'S WORLD CUP

Lisa De Vanna (11) and Heather Garriock of Australia (7) tussle with Elaine of Brazil in the quarter-final.

THE HISTORY OF THE WOMEN'S WORLD CUP

2007 FINAL

 GERMANY 2-0 BRAZIL

A crowd of 31,000 people packed into the stadium and they were certainly in for a treat. As they waited for the referee, Tammy Ogston from Australia, to start the game, the Germans stood in a line, calm and focused, while the Brazilians bounced around on their heels impatiently. They had contrasting approaches and contrasting styles, but both teams had reason to feel confident. On their journey to the final in Shanghai, the Germans had scored 19 goals yet hadn't conceded a single one – a record that still hasn't been bettered. The Brazilians had scored almost as many – 17 – but had only let in two. Before the game, German coach Silvia Neid, who had been Tina Theune-Meyer's assistant when Germany had won the previous tournament, acknowledged that her side couldn't match the Brazilians player for player, but, she said, 'What we have to do is give them as little space as possible.'

She was undoubtedly right and that, indeed, is what Germany did, but the South Americans fairly swiftly discovered a way of slipping through the German defence, with Daniela hitting the post for Brazil early on. However, German Kerstin Garefrekes found the side netting and Sandra Smisek had a shot that went over the bar. At half-time it was 0-0, but after seven minutes back on the field Kerstin Stegemann sent a long pass into Brazil's box, Smisek pushed it back to captain Birgit Prinz, who tapped it in – 1-0 to Germany. Then the action switched to the other end, where an under-pressure Linda Bresonik felled Cristiane in the German area and gave away a penalty. Of course, it was Marta, World Cup wonder and tournament top scorer with seven goals, who stepped up. And it was Germany's goalkeeper Nadine Angerer who faced her and, miraculously for the Germans, saved her 64th-minute shot. Then three minutes later, Angerer also saved a dangerous free kick from Daniela, pushing it onto the post. The score remained 1-0 until the 86th minute, when Simone Laudehr's head got on the end of an in-swinging corner from Renate Lingor's corner. It was a late goal from the 21-year-old, but it assured Germany's win. As Neid said afterwards, for Germany, 'It was the perfect tournament.'

The Hongkou Football Stadium, in Shanghai, China played host to the 2007 final.

The 2-0 scoreline reflected a little harshly on Brazil though. Silvia Neid's disciplined force had successfully stifled Jorge Barcellos' flair players, particularly Marta, who found it virtually impossible to link up effectively with the rest of her team and, in particular, to get a good shot on goal. Mind you, there was some consolation for Marta in that, despite being unable to add to her tally in the final, not only did she win the Golden Boot for scoring those seven goals, she also won the tournament's Golden Ball for the best player. The Silver Boot went to USA's Abby Wambach, who netted six times, as did the Bronze Boot, Sweden's Ragnhild Gulbrandsen, while the Germany's Birgit Prinz won the Silver Ball and Brazil's Cristiane the bronze.

MAGIC MOMENT

When she lifted the trophy in the Shanghai Hongkou Football Stadium it was truly a magic moment for Birgit Prinz. Not only was Germany the first country to retain the Women's World Cup, but also she was the first player to play in three World Cup finals – in 1995, 2003 and 2007.

WWC CHINA 2007 | FINAL

▼ Germany's goalkeeper Nadine Angerer reacts after saving Marta's penalty in the final.

▲ Hundreds of German supporters welcomed the team back home as they celebrated on the balcony of Frankfurt's city hall with the World Cup trophy.

113

THE HISTORY OF THE WOMEN'S WORLD CUP

WOMEN'S WORLD CUP GERMANY 2011

Germany had won the 2003 and 2007 Women's World Cup tournaments and were hosting the 2011 edition. The tried and trusted format of 16 teams in four groups of four was used again, but in a break with previous tournaments, on matchdays each stadium would be the venue for just the one game. A record nine stadiums in nine different cities were used – Augsburg, Berlin, Bochum, Dresden, Frankfurt, Leverkusen, Mönchengladbach, Sinsheim and Wolfsburg – with the final itself being played in Frankfurt.

The mascot was a cat called Karla Kick and at the unveiling ceremony, former German player Steffi Jones, who was president of FIFA's Women's World Cup 2011 organising committee, said, 'Our mascot fully conveys the attributes of women's football, namely passion, enjoyment and dynamism.' She was also very sweet.

China were noticeable by their absence from Germany 2011. The 2010 AFC Women's Asian Cup offered three qualification slots, but China had lost to the North Koreans in the semi-finals and then the Japanese in the third-place play-off. In the group stage the spotlight fell firmly on one of those Asian teams responsible for China staying at home for the first and so far only time: Japan.

In March that year, a devastating earthquake and tsunami had damaged Japan's Fukushima Daiichi nuclear power plant and three nuclear reactors went into meltdown. Football was suspended and the team debated pulling out of the World Cup, although eventually they decided to go. Two Japanese players – Karina Maruyama and Aya Sameshima – were former workers at the plant, and at their games against New Zealand and England the Japanese unfurled a banner with the heartfelt message: 'To our friends around the world thank you for your support.'

WWC GERMANY 2011

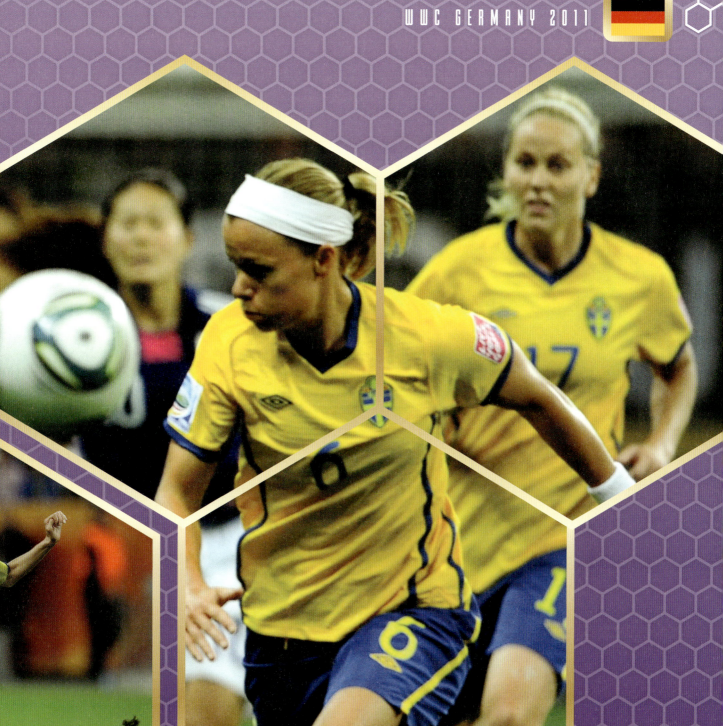

THE HISTORY OF THE WOMEN'S WORLD CUP

GROUP STAGE

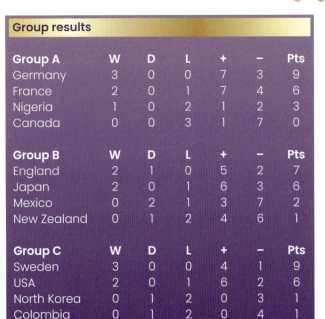

Group results

Group A	W	D	L	+	−	Pts
Germany	3	0	0	7	3	9
France	2	0	1	7	4	6
Nigeria	1	0	2	1	2	3
Canada	0	0	3	1	7	0

Group B	W	D	L	+	−	Pts
England	2	1	0	5	2	7
Japan	2	0	1	6	3	6
Mexico	0	2	1	3	7	2
New Zealand	0	1	2	4	6	1

Group C	W	D	L	+	−	Pts
Sweden	3	0	0	4	1	9
USA	2	0	1	6	2	6
North Korea	0	1	2	0	3	1
Colombia	0	1	2	0	4	1

Group D	W	D	L	+	−	Pts
Brazil	3	0	0	7	0	9
Australia	2	0	1	5	4	6
Norway	1	0	2	2	5	3
Equatorial Guinea	0	0	3	2	7	0

The first game of group A was France versus Nigeria in Sinsheim, which France duly won, 1-0. The second was the 150th game of the Women's World Cup and it featured Germany against Canada in Berlin. Although coach Silvia Neid was clear she wanted to concentrate on the current tournament, Germany were defending champions and looking to lift the trophy for a third consecutive time. They got off to good start by beating Canada, 2-1, but despite a broken nose the Canadian skipper Christine Sinclair scored from a free kick to put a stop to German goalkeeper Nadine Angerer's record 622 World Cup minutes without conceding. During the game against Nigeria, German legend Birgit Prinz' illustrious World Cup career was halted by injury, but in the end Germany were top of the group on nine points and Canada bottom on zero. France also went through, beating Canada as well as Nigeria, but losing 4-2 to the Germans.

In Group B, England drew 1-1 with Mexico, but beat New Zealand 2-1 and Japan 2-0, a game that saw Ellen White and Rachel Yankey both score excellent goals. That meant England qualified first, finishing on seven points, one point above Japan, who beat not only New Zealand, but also Mexico. The scoreline in the latter was 4-0, with Japan's Homare Sawa, destined to be the big name at this World Cup, getting a hat-trick. Unfortunately for them, Mexico, who had 16-year-old Cecilia Santiago in goal, and New Zealand, whose goalkeeper, Jenny Bindon, at 38 was somewhat older, were out.

When it came to Group C, dubbed this tournament's group of death, the experienced Swedish side took the maximum nine points. They beat newbies Colombia, only the third South American team to appear in the Women's World Cup finals, 1-0, with a Jessica Landström goal. The scoreline was the same against North Korea, this time the goal coming from Lisa Dahlkvist. When they played USA it was 2-1 to Sweden, Dahlkvist scoring again followed by an own goal from Amy Le Peilbet, with Abby Wambach's second half strike not enough to salvage the game. Sweden and USA progressed; Colombia and North Korea left the competition having failed to score at all.

Brazil recorded three straight wins in Group D: 3-0 against Equatorial Guinea, who were former African champions but had never qualified for the Women's World Cup before – Érika got one, Cristiane two; 1-0 against Australia – the goal came from Rosana; and 3-0 against Norway, a game in which Rosana fired in one and Marta two. So Brazil were through, but who would join them? Former champions Norway, now coached by a woman, Eli Landsem, for the first time, would have been a good bet, but although they triumphed over Equatorial Guinea thanks to a late goal from Emilie Haavi, Australia got the better of them when, after an early goal from Norwegian Elise Thorsnes, Australian star Kyah Simon hit two. It was something of a shock, but Norway were out and Australia followed Brazil into the knockout stage

FACT FOCUS

Sweden had also come third in 1991, so by beating France in the 2011 play-off they were picking up the 'bronze medal', as it were, for the second time. Add that to their 2003 runners-up position and Sweden was the most successful Women's World Cup nation that hadn't won the trophy itself.

WWC GERMANY 2011 | GROUP AND KNOCKOUT STAGES

KNOCKOUT STAGE

Knockout results

Quarter-finals
(after extra-time) Japan	1-0	Germany
(on penalties) France	4-3	England
Sweden	3-1	Australia
(on penalties) USA	5-3	Brazil

Semi-finals
Japan	3-1	Sweden
USA	3-1	France

Third-place play-off
Sweden	2-1	France

For the first quarter-final, in Wolfsburg, Germany lined up against Japan. The Germans were skilled and well prepared, but just couldn't score, while the Japanese defended valiantly, particularly goalie Ayumi Kaihori. It was 0-0 after 90 minutes so went to extra-time. The decisive moment came in the 108th minute, when Karina Maruyama slid the ball home from a tight angle. It remained 1-0 to Japan and, to most people's shock, Germany's departed from the tournament.

England had last beaten France in 1974, but in Leverkusen it looked like the jinx was over when Jill Scott scored after 59 minutes. However, just before full-time – in the 88th minute – Élise Bussaglia levelled and at 1-1 it went to extra-time. When that produced no further goals, it was penalties. English keeper Karen Bardsley saved Camille Abily's shot, but her teammates Claire Rafferty and Faye White both missed. The French were in the semi-finals.

The young Australian side never gave up in their Augsburg quarter-final against Sweden, but in truth the Scandinavians were more experienced and their early goals – Therese Sjögran after 11 minutes and Lisa Dahlkvist after 16 – were crucial. Australia's Ellyse Perry responded just before half-time, making it 2-1 to Sweden. However, when they returned, Lotta Schelin capitalised on a poor back pass and it ended 3-1 – the only one of these quarter-finals not to go to extra-time. The Australians' dream was over. The Swedes' lived on.

Brazil versus USA in Dresden was certainly dramatic. After two minutes Daiane's own goal gifted USA the lead. It wasn't all plain sailing for the Americans, though, as Rachel Buehler was sent off for a foul on Marta. The Brazilians were awarded a penalty. Hope Solo saved Cristiane's shot, but the referee ordered a retake. This time Marta herself stepped up – and converted. It was 1-1 after normal time and 2-2 after extra-time, thanks to goals from Marta again and Abby Wambach. The Americans scored all their penalties, but it wasn't Daiane's day as Solo saved her spot-kick to put USA through.

After ten minutes of the Frankfurt semi-final Sweden were ahead through Josefine Öqvist, but before another ten minutes were up Japan's Nahomi Kawasumi had responded. The Japanese continued to press, but it remained 1-1 until the hour mark, when Homare Sawa's header hit the back of the net, followed four minutes later by another from Kawasumi. Japan were in the final.

In the other semi-final, USA's Lauren Cheney scored after only nine minutes, but despite their constant pressure it took France until the 55th minute to equalise Sonia Bompastor's speculative shot. USA raised their game and Abby Wambach put them ahead with a 79th-minute header. Three minutes later Alex Morgan then chipped the French keeper, Bérangère Sapowicz, to confirm USA's final place.

So Sweden and France played off for third place, and Sweden initially went ahead went when Lotta Schelin blasted in a shot. France were unlucky to lose goalie Sapowicz and midfielder Louisa Nécib to injuries, but Nécib's replacement, Élodie Thomis, equalised after 56 minutes. It was then Sweden's turn to lose a player, although Öqvist was sent off, but 29-year-old Marie Hammerstrom scored a superb goal to cement Sweden's third place.

▲ Lotte Schlein scored two goals in the 2011 finals to help Sweden to secure a third-place position.

THE HISTORY OF THE WOMEN'S WORLD CUP

Japan's striker Shinobu Ohno (L) races Sweden's defender Sara Thunebro for the ball during semi-final match in Frankfurt.

THE HISTORY OF THE WOMEN'S WORLD CUP

▼ **Homare Sawa** scored the crucial equaliser in the final. She was Japan's captain and had been their inspiration throughout their incredible World Cup journey.

120

WWC GERMANY 2011 | FINAL

2011 FINAL

 JAPAN 3-1 USA

(on penalties)

▲ Frankfurt's Commerzbank Arena, venue for the first UEFA Women's Cup (later called Champions League) in 2002 and the 2011 World Cup final.

When USA and Japan met in the Commerzbank Arena in Frankfurt in front of a crowd of almost 49,000, it was generally acknowledged to be the most exciting final – in fact, possibly the most exciting match – that the Women's World Cup had produced to date. USA were undoubtedly the favourites, and twice USA went ahead and it looked as though it was all over for Japan. However, twice Japan came back and in fact, much to the delight of spectators, the whole game was characterised by this type of action and corresponding reaction.

Despite being known for their smooth passing game, from the kick-off it looked as though Japan were struggling with their nerves, while USA got stuck in immediately, but even so there was no score in the first half. USA's Alex Morgan, who had come on for Lauren Cheney after the break, got the first goal on 69 minutes, but 12 minutes later Aya Miyama responded and forced the game into extra-time, where the same pattern repeated itself. In the 104th minute Abby Wambach put USA back in the lead, but this time it was 13 minutes before Homare Sawa balanced the scoreline again. After another three minutes it was still 2-2 and referee Bibiana Steinhaus from Germany blew her whistle to signal that there would now be a penalty shoot-out.

USA's Shannon Boxx stepped up to the spot first, but Ayumi Kaihori stuck out her foot to save her shot and then Miyama scored. Carli Lloyd's penalty went straight over the top post, although Hope Solo kept out Yūki Nagasato. Kaihori batted away Tobin Heath's attempt, but Solo couldn't stop Mizuho Sakaguchi. Abby Wambach scored to keep USA dreams alive, but when Saki Kumagai hit her shot beyond Solo's reach and firmly into back of the net it was all over, 3-1 to the Japanese, and Japan, coached by Norio Sasaki, had become the first Asian team – men or women – to win a World Cup.

Even though Japan was ranked fourth in the world, few pundits had expected them to emerge from the knockout stages, let alone win the whole tournament, so it was an incredible upset, not to mention an incredible achievement. Kaihori was declared player of the match and for her five tournament goals Homare Sawa received the Golden Boot (Marta and Wambach both finished on four goals) and she was awarded the Golden Ball too.

Of course, the USA players and coach Pia Sundhage, the former Swedish player, were devastated to lose, but USA forward Abby Wambach was later quoted as saying with great humility that she thought perhaps, because of the earthquake and the tsunami that had claimed 20,000 lives earlier that year, Japan as a nation needed the Japanese women's team to lift the World Cup more than USA did. She said, 'The thought that their success will bring happiness and hope to the Japanese people is a consolation.'

MAGIC MOMENT

As one indicator of the profile and status of the Women's World Cup, for the 2011 tournament Panini produced one of its popular sticker albums for the first time. Distributed only in Germany, the sticker pack sold out and had to be reprinted, and completed albums are now highly sought after and very valuable.

THE HISTORY OF THE WOMEN'S WORLD CUP

WOMEN'S WORLD CUP CANADA 2015

In 2015 the Women's World Cup came to Canada. Six stadiums in six cities (in five different time zones) were used for the tournament — Edmonton, Moncton (a small city in the east), Montreal, Ottawa, Vancouver and Winnipeg, although not Toronto, Canada's largest city, because it was hosting the Pan-American Games that year. In a departure from previous events, because of the size of the country and the distances involved, each group's initial games were centred on one location.

However, more significantly, for the first time the number of teams rose from 16 to 24. Those teams were still divided into groups of four, but there was a new round of 16, before the usual quarter-finals, semi-finals and final. The increase in the number of qualifying teams meant that eight of the sides had not been to a World Cup before: the Netherlands, Spain and Switzerland from Europe; Thailand from Asia; Cameroon and Côte d'Ivoire from Africa; Costa Rica from Central America; and Ecuador from South America. When the squads were announced, though, there were some familiar names in the line-ups as Brazil's Formiga and Japan's Homare Sawa were both heading to the World Cup for the sixth time – a record for the women's and the men's game.

The mascot for the event, a cheery snowy owl wearing what looked like a lot of mascara, was called Shuéme. Other innovations included Hawk Eye goal-line technology, which was used for the first time, and this was also the first World Cup – again, men's or women's – where all the games were played on astroturf.

WWC CANADA 2015

THE HISTORY OF THE WOMEN'S WORLD CUP

GROUP STAGE

Home side Canada made heavy weather of a youthful Chinese team, but a penalty from legend Christine Sinclair in the 92nd minute gave them the 1-0 win. They only drew with New Zealand and Netherlands, but still managed to top Group A with five points. China beat Netherlands, giving them four points and second place, while Netherlands was one of best third-placed teams overall so they went through.

Group B contained two heavyweights and two newbies. Côte d'Ivoire struggled to win a match, but did score three goals. Thailand's only victory was against Côte d'Ivoire, 3-2, but they lost 4-0 to both Germany and Norway. Germany and Norway drew 1-1 and finished on seven points each, but Germany came top on goal difference – they had beaten Côte d'Ivoire 10-0 which helped.

Japan's defence of their title began well with a 1-0 victory over Switzerland, thanks to a 29th-minute penalty from skipper Aya Miyama. Japan also beat Ecuador – coached by 26-year-old Vanessa Arauz, the youngest coach in Women's World Cup history – 1-0 and Cameroon 2-1, which gave them nine points. First-timers Cameroon, came second after conquering Switzerland 2-1 and Ecuador with a decisive scoreline of 6-0. However, Switzerland in third also progressed.

In Group D USA dropped a couple of points by drawing 0-0 with Sweden, but secured seven points with wins in the matches versus Australia, 3-1, and Nigeria, 1-0. Second-placed Australia did well to go through to the next stage on four points, gained from a 2-0 win over Nigeria and a 1-1 draw with Sweden. The Scandinavians' three points from their three draws meant they scraped across the line as well.

In the opening game of Group E, Brazil beat South Korea 2-0 after 37-year-old Formiga became the oldest woman to score in a World Cup, and Marta put away a penalty to score her 15th World Cup goal – a record she had previously shared with Birgit Prinz. Brazil walked their other two games, beating both Spain and Costa Rica 1-0, and their place in the next round was assured. There was a gap to South Korea, who drew with Costa Rica, 2-2, and bested Spain, 2-1, giving them four points. Costa Rica and Spain, both new to the tournament, gained valuable experience on the international stage, but no points.

Group F was quite tight. France and England met in the first game and thanks to Eugénie Le Sommer the French emerged the victors, 1-0, which prolonged France's 41-year unbeaten run against England. Both nations then beat Mexico, 5-0 for France and 2-1 for England, but France lost to Colombia, 2-0, while England managed a 2-1 win over the Colombians. When the dust settled, France was top with six points, due to goal difference, followed by England, also on six points. However, Colombia on four went through, too, and Mexico missed out.

Group results

Group A	W	D	L	+	–	Pts
Canada	1	2	0	2	1	5
China	1	1	1	3	3	4
Netherlands	1	1	1	2	2	4
New Zealand	0	2	1	2	3	2

Group B	W	D	L	+	–	Pts
Germany	2	1	0	15	1	7
Norway	2	1	0	8	2	7
Thailand	1	0	2	3	10	3
Côte d'Ivoire	0	0	3	3	16	0

Group C	W	D	L	+	–	Pts
Japan	3	0	0	4	1	9
Cameroon	2	0	1	9	3	6
Switzerland	1	0	2	11	4	3
Ecuador	0	0	3	1	17	0

Group D	W	D	L	+	–	Pts
USA	2	1	0	4	1	7
Australia	1	1	1	4	4	4
Sweden	0	3	0	4	4	3
Nigeria	0	1	2	3	6	1

Group E	W	D	L	+	–	Pts
Brazil	3	0	0	4	0	9
South Korea	1	1	1	4	5	4
Costa Rica	0	2	1	3	4	2
Spain	0	1	2	2	4	1

Group F	W	D	L	+	–	Pts
France	2	0	1	6	2	6
England	2	0	1	4	3	6
Colombia	1	1	1	4	3	4
Mexico	0	1	2	2	8	1

WWC CANADA 2015 | GROUP STAGES | ROUND OF 16

ROUND OF 16

Knockout results

Round of 16

Germany	4-1	Sweden
China	1-0	Cameroon
Australia	1-0	Brazil
France	3-0	South Korea
Canada	1-0	Switzerland
England	2-1	Norway
USA	2-0	Colombia
Japan	2-1	Netherlands

The new round of 16 was a simple knockout format and most of the eight games went to form, although in some the outcome was not quite as anticipated. China versus Cameroon fell into the first category, although the African side, which featured several members who played overseas – Ajara Nchout in USA, Gaëlle Enganamouit in Sweden – gave an excellent account of themselves. At the final whistle, all that stood between the two teams was Wang Shansam's side-footed, close-range shot in the 12th minute, so China clinched it 1-0.

Germany and Sweden had history – Silvia Neid, in charge of Germany, and Pia Sundhage, who helmed Sweden, had played in the same era and met as coaches too – but the Germans looked forward not back. Anja Mittag opened the scoring for them after 24 minutes, followed by Célia Šašić, who grabbed two, one a penalty. Sweden's Linda Sembrant pulled one back in the 82nd minute, but it was too late and Dzsenifer Marozsán got another in the 88th minute to make it a very decisive 4-1 win for Germany.

Brazil had got the better of Australia in previous World Cup tournaments and this was a closely fought meeting, with Australian goalkeeper Lydia Williams crucial to keeping her team in the game by successfully repelling shots from Cristiane, Marta and Formiga. It was 0-0 until ten minutes before the end when super-sub Kyah Simon made it 1-0 to Australia. The Brazilians were gone.

France made pretty light work of knocking out South Korea. The Asian side's squad included several members of its successful Under-17 and Under-20 teams, but talismanic Ji So Yun was out injured, and two goals from Marie-Laure Delie and one from Élodie Thomis assured the French victory.

Canada versus Switzerland had verve and drama, with both goalies, Erin McLeod for Canada and Gaëlle Thalmann her Swiss counterpart, making crucial saves, but much to the joy of the 54,000-strong home crowd it was settled in the 52nd minute when a goal from Josée Bélanger took Canada through.

Norway edged the possession and got more shots in than England. They also broke the deadlock to score first, after 54 minutes, courtesy of 34-year-old veteran Solveig Gulbrandsen, who had retired in 2010, but was back to help out her national team. However, captain Steph Houghton quickly retaliated and then Lucy Bronze hit one of the best goals of the tournament, so it finished 2-1 to England.

USA had no real trouble dispatching Colombia, particularly when the South Americans' 20-year-old goalkeeper, Catalina Pérez, who was filling in for their suspended first-choice goalie, was sent off after she brought down USA's Alex Morgan. Abby Wambach missed the ensuing penalty, but Morgan and Carli Lloyd both got goals and, although the young Colombians had impressed, it finished 2-0 to USA.

Netherlands had done well to get this far, but they faced an on-form Japan who were ahead after ten minutes thanks to right-back Saori Ariyoshi. Japan's second goal, which showcased Mizuho Sakaguchi's superb finishing, came at 78 minutes and, although Netherlands' Kirsten van de Ven made it 2-1 in the dying minutes, the Japanese held on for the win. The 16 were now down to eight.

USA legends Abby Wambach and Hope Solo wave goodbye. They both played their last World Cup game in the 2015 final.

THE HISTORY OF THE WOMEN'S WORLD CUP

QUARTER-FINALS AND SEMI-FINALS

Knockout results

Quarter-finals
(on penalties) Germany	5-4	France
USA	1-0	China
Japan	1-0	Australia
England	2-1	Canada

Semi-finals
Japan	2-1	England
USA	2-0	Germany

Third-place play-off
(after extra-time) England	1-0	Germany

France and Germany met in Montreal for the first quarter-final and in the first half the French managed to hold the Germans back and were rewarded with a Louisa Nécib goal 20 minutes after the restart. However, six minutes from full-time a penalty was given against them, which Célia Šašić calmly converted. After extra time it was still 1-1, so the teams lined up for penalties. Germany hit five out of five and veteran goalkeeper Nadine Angerer saved Claire Lavogez' shot with her knee, so Germany were through to the next round.

USA had reached the semi-finals in all six previous tournaments, but could China prevent them reaching a seventh? USA were missing Megan Rapinoe and Lauren Holiday, but that didn't stop them dominating their opponents, although they didn't score until the second half when Carli Lloyd headed home. You couldn't fault the Chinese for effort, particularly not keeper Wang Fei, but it wasn't their day. It ended 1-0 to USA.

Australia were a developing side, Japan were experienced, and they had recently met in World Cup qualifier, the AFC Women's Asian Cup. On that occasion Japan had emerged the victors and in this quarter-final the result was the same. Goalkeeper Lydia Williams had kept them in it and Sam Kerr had come close, but Australia ultimately succumbed to a late goal from Japanese sub Mana Iwabuchi.

In the other quarter-final hosts Canada met England. The atmosphere in the stadium was, by all accounts, electric, but that soon fizzled away, because Jodie Taylor and Lucy Bronze scored for England before 15 minutes were up. The legendary Christine Sinclair responded just before half-time, but there were no goals in the second half and the final result was 2-1 to England. A distraught Canada were out.

Two penalties and an own goal was the story of the first semi-final. At 33 minutes the Japanese had the first chance to score from the spot. Aya Miyama stepped up and put it away, but seven minutes later it was England's turn and Fara Williams didn't falter either. At 1-1 it went back and forth until injury time, when Laura Bassett botched an intercept and beat her own keeper. Japan were heading for the final.

USA and Germany were the top-ranked teams and 51,000 came to watch this semi-final, in which penalties also proved crucial. In the German goal Angerer repelled shots from USA's Alex Morgan and Julie Johnston in the first half. In the second half both sides were awarded penalties in the space of six minutes. Šašić missed hers for Germany, but Lloyd made sure she put hers away for USA and Kelley O'Hara prodded home another, making it 2-0 plus and a place in the final for USA.

It was left to England and Germany to fight it out for third place. There were a few thrills and spills, and Germany generally had the best of it, but 0-0 meant it went to extra-time. In the 108th minute Germany's Tabea Kemme brought down England sub Lianne Sanderson in the box, the referee pointed to the spot and Fara Williams converted the penalty. It was 1-0 to England.

FACT FOCUS

The referee who awarded England the penalty that settled the third-place play-off was Ri Hyang Ok, who was the first former Women's World Cup player to referee at the tournament. She had been a member of the North Korea team that took part in the 1999 and 2003 competitions.

WWC CANADA 2015 | QUARTER-FINALS AND SEMI-FINALS

Goalkeeper Fei Wang of China is challenged by USA's Carli Lloyd (10) and Alex Morgan (13) in their quarter-final match.

▲ Germany's Lena Petermann escapes the attentions of the English defence in the third-place match.

WWC CANADA 2015 | QUARTER-FINALS AND SEMI-FINALS

THE HISTORY OF THE WOMEN'S WORLD CUP

2015 FINAL

USA 5-2 JAPAN

Finals aren't always great spectacles, but this one, between USA and Japan, in Vancouver, in front of over 53,000 people, certainly was – from two minutes 35 seconds in, when the American captain Carli Lloyd hit her first goal of the game. Lloyd's next came after five minutes. She then passed the baton to teammate Lauren Holiday, who got on the scoresheet at 14 minutes. Lloyd completed her hat-trick – the first hat-trick ever scored in a Women's World Cup final – on the 16-minute mark, when she unleashed a blistering shot from the centre circle. It flew past Japanese keeper Ayumi Kaihori, who had drifted off her line, and into the back of the net.

The Japanese were stunned – after just over a quarter of an hour they were 4-0 down. Could they come back from that scoreline? They gave it a go and in the 27th minute Japanese striker Yūki Ōgimi managed to keep Julie Johnston at bay in the box to shoot past USA goalie Hope Solo. So it was 4-1 when they went in for the break and shortly after they came out again it was 4-2. Seven minutes after the restart, the aforementioned Julie Johnston accidentally headed Japanese skipper Aya Miyama's free kick past Solo and into the back of her own net.

In 2011, USA had made the mistake of allowing Japan back into the game, not once, but twice, so they were determined not to let the same thing to happen again and two minutes after that, in the 54th minute, Tobin Heath side-footed the ball to make it 5-2 to USA and restore their three-goal margin, a margin they held on to until referee Kateryna Monzul from Ukraine blew the final whistle. Lloyd and Heath had both missed their 2011 shoot-out penalties. They had certainly redeemed themselves and USA had achieved their third World Cup, the only nation to have done so, while Japan, much to their disappointment, had failed to win a second successive tournament.

Lloyd's hat-trick alone was quite a feat and one of only three ever scored in the knockout stages of the tournament – fellow Americans Michelle Akers and Carin Jennings were responsible for the other two, both back in 1999 – but 17 hat-

Amid desperate defending, Japan goalkeeper Ayumi Kaihori thwarts a USA attack in the 2015 final.

tricks in total have been scored during the group stages of the competition.

As a footnote, the Women's World Cup 2015 was played exclusively on astroturf and before the tournament began a group of top players, including Brazil's Marta, USA's Abby Wambach, Germany's Nadine Angerer, Australia's Sam Kerr and South Korea's Ji So Yun, filed a petition in a Canadian court claiming gender discrimination. This was on the grounds that men's World Cup matches were always played on grass, which the women argued was much less physically damaging than playing on an artificial surface. They dropped the case when it became clear that the competition would go ahead on astro, but a point about parity had been made.

MAGIC MOMENT

When Christie Rampone came on late in the final it marked the end of a remarkable career. She had quite a collection of medals, including a 1999 winners' medal, and it was 11 days after she had celebrated her 40th birthday, making her the oldest player to take to the field in any Women's World Cup.

WWC CANADA 2015 | FINALS

Megan Rapinoe (15) celebrates while hat-trick hero and USA captain Carli Lloyd raises the World Cup trophy.

THE HISTORY OF THE WOMEN'S WORLD CUP

WOMEN'S WORLD CUP FRANCE 2019

Since that first tournament in China in 1991, each successive Women's World Cup had built enthusiasm, respect and status for women's football, as well as an ever-larger number of interested spectators, and in 2019 the games were all broadcast, to a combined TV audience of 1.12 billion.

France was the host and the matches were played in stadiums clustered in the north of the country – Paris, Le Havre, Reims, Rennes and Valenciennes – and the south-east – Grenoble, Lyon, Montpellier and Nice. A single stadium – the Stade de Lyon – was the venue for both the semi-finals and the final itself.

The format of six groups of four teams, with either two or three teams going through to a round of 16, was retained from 2015, but among those gathered in France were four nations which hadn't qualified for a Women's World Cup before and for whom a global tournament was a whole new experience: Chile, Jamaica, Scotland and South Africa (although South Africa had previously been to the Olympic Games).

In fact, while the Women's World Cup 2019 was taking place, FIFA suggested that the number of participants should be increased yet again, from 24 to 32, to encourage countries that didn't traditionally have a women's team to develop one, and it was agreed that this would take effect in 2023.

The official mascot – a chicken in a suitably Gallic blue-and-white striped shirt – was called Ettie and this tournament had an official slogan, too. It was 'Dare to shine' – and many of the teams and players did just that, but particularly the undoubted star of the show, USA's Megan Rapinoe.

WWC FRANCE 2019

THE HISTORY OF THE WOMEN'S WORLD CUP

GROUP STAGE

After an opening ceremony featuring acrobats and fireworks, France made a cracking start to Group A's games, beating South Korea 4-0 on a chilly evening in Paris. The goals came from Eugénie Le Sommer, Wendie Renard, who bagged a brace, and Amandine Henry. France's Griedge Mbock Bathy also had a beautifully struck shot disallowed by VAR – the first time that had happened in the Women's World Cup. France continued their winning form, triumphing over Nigeria 1-0 and Norway 2-1 to top the group. The Norwegians won their other two games to make second place, while the Nigerians managed to beat South Korea 2-0, so also went through as one of the best third-placed teams

In Group B, the Germans also took maximum points, beating China and Spain 1-0, and South Africa 4-0. This was a group where three teams qualified for the next round, and China and Spain both beat South Africa, 1-0 and 3-1 respectively, so they both finished up with four points and moved forward.

In Group C, three teams finished on six points, so Italy, Australia and Brazil all progressed. The closest scoreline was Australia's 3-2 victory over Brazil, but it was against Brazil that Italy dropped points, that encounter ending 1-0 to Brazil. The other team in the group was Jamaica.

In Group D, England beat Scotland 2-1, thanks to a 14-minute penalty converted by Nikita Parris and a goal from Ellen White just before half-time, although Scotland's Claire Emslie pulled one back in the 80th minute. England also conquered Japan, 2-0, and Argentina, 1-0, to top the group. Japan drew with Argentina and beat Scotland, whereas Argentina could only manage a draw with Scotland. The game ended 3-3 even though Scotland was leading 3-0 after 70 minutes. All that meant Japan came second and was into the round of 16.

Kadeisha Buchanan's header dead on half-time was all that separated the Canadians from the Cameroonians in the opening game in Group E. Netherlands also managed to beat Cameroon – it was a comfortable 3-1 victory – but Cameroon bested New Zealand, 2-1, leaving the Africans in third with three points. This was good enough to send them through, along with first-placed Netherlands and second-placed Japan.

You couldn't fault USA. They won all their games – which included a 13-0 drubbing of Thailand – to finish top in Group F and sail through to the next round. Sweden's 5-1 scoreline against Thailand wasn't quite so convincing, but they also beat Chile 2-0 and that secured them second place in the group. Although Chile versus Thailand ended 2-0 to Chile, it wasn't enough to give the South Americans a best third-placed teams spot, so their tournament was over, but at least they had gained some valuable experience on the international stage.

Group results

Group A	W	D	L	+	−	Pts
France	3	0	0	7	1	9
Norway	2	0	1	6	3	6
Nigeria	1	0	2	2	4	3
South Korea	0	0	3	1	8	0

Group B	W	D	L	+	−	Pts
Germany	3	0	0	6	0	9
Spain	1	1	1	3	2	4
China	1	1	1	1	1	4
South Africa	0	0	3	1	8	0

Group C	W	D	L	+	−	Pts
Italy	2	0	1	7	2	6
Australia	2	0	1	8	5	6
Brazil	2	0	1	6	3	6
Jamaica	0	0	3	1	12	0

Group D	W	D	L	+	−	Pts
England	3	0	0	5	1	9
Japan	1	1	1	2	3	4
Argentina	0	2	1	3	4	2
Scotland	0	1	2	5	7	1

Group E	W	D	L	+	−	Pts
Netherlands	3	0	0	6	2	9
Canada	2	0	1	4	2	6
Cameroon	1	0	2	3	5	3
New Zealand	0	0	3	1	5	0

Group F	W	D	L	+	−	Pts
USA	3	0	0	18	0	9
Sweden	2	0	1	7	3	6
China	1	0	2	2	5	3
Thailand	0	0	3	1	20	0

WWC FRANCE 2019 | GROUP STAGES | ROUND OF 16

ROUND OF 16

Knockout results

Round of 16

Germany	3-0	Nigeria
(on penalties) Norway	4-1	Australia
England	3-0	Cameroon
(after extra-time) France	2-1	Brazil
USA	2-1	Spain
Sweden	1-0	Canada
Italy	2-0	China
Netherlands	2-1	Japan

On paper, Germany versus Nigeria looked like it would be a walkover for the highly ranked Europeans, but most of the African team were based abroad and there was quality in their side. They gave their opponents a run for their money, but two German goals in the first half – one a header from captain Alexandra Popp, the other a penalty put away by Sara Däbritz – followed by a Nigerian defensive error, which Germany's Lea Schüller exploited, were decisive and it ended 3-0.

The Australians' motto was 'Never say die' and this game exemplified that. Norway were ahead on the half-hour mark with a goal from Isabell Herlovsen, but Australia couldn't equalise until the 83rd minute when Elise Kellond-Knight scored from a corner. At 1-1 it went to extra-time. However, Australian skipper Sam Kerr missed, Emily Gielnik's shot was saved and ultimately they lost 4-1.

England versus Cameroon was dominated by several contested VAR decisions, with the Africans holding up play twice – when an Ellen White goal for England that had been flagged offside was allowed to stand by VAR and when a blistering shot from Cameroon's Ajara Nchout was disallowed by VAR. The game ended 3-0 to England and Cameroon were going home.

In their game against the Brazilians, the French also had a goal ruled ineligible by VAR, but after the break Valérie Gauvin made it 1-0 to France. Brazil's Thaisa countered quickly, so it was 1-1 at full-time. The Brazilian team was packed with experienced players, but perhaps their age was a factor as it went to extra-time, because they weren't able to come back when the French captain Amandine Henry scored the winner in the 107th minute.

When they gave away a penalty and USA's Megan Rapinoe converted it in the seventh minute it wasn't quite the start Spain were hoping for. However, two minutes later Jennifer Hermoso equalised – the first goal USA had conceded in 317 minutes of open play – and Spain managed to keep it at 1-1 until 15 minutes from the end, when they gave away a second penalty and Rapinoe converted it once again. It finished 2-1 to USA.

Leading 1-0 after Stina Blackstenius' 55th-minute toe poke, it looked like an easy win for Sweden against a youthful Canadian side. In the 69th minute, though, VAR identified a handball by Sweden's Kosovare Asllani and Canada had the chance to equalise. Janine Beckie stepped up, but keeper Hedvig Lindahl dived with determination to save her penalty and it stayed 1-0 to Sweden.

Having topped their group Italy were riding high and here they scored once in each half, first through Valentina Giacinti and then Aurora Galli. China, on the other hand, while generally maintaining a tight defence had real issues scoring and couldn't respond to the Italians, so 2-0 to Italy was the final score.

This game hinged on a last-minute penalty, awarded against Japan's Saki Kumgai, who was deemed to have handled in the area. Up until then Japan versus Netherlands had been relatively evenly matched. Perhaps the Japanese had just edged it, but the scoreline stood at 1-1. Lieke Martens dispatched the penalty confidently to make it 2-1 to Netherlands and put Japan out.

FACT FOCUS

At this World Cup Brazil's Formiga surpassed USA's Christie Rampone to become the oldest player to take to the field – she was 41 years and 98 days old. She also became the first player to play in seven World Cup tournaments. Amazingly, when she made her Women's World Cup debut 150 France 2019 players weren't even born!

THE HISTORY OF THE WOMEN'S WORLD CUP

QUARTER-FINALS AND SEMI-FINALS

Knockout results

Quarter-finals
England	3-0	Norway
USA	2-1	France
Netherlands	2-0	Italy
Sweden	2-1	Germany

Semi-finals
USA	2-1	England
Netherlands	1-0	Sweden

Third-place play-off
Sweden	2-1	England

The quarter-finals would turn eight into four and they kicked off with England making short work of Norway. England's Jill Scott scored the tournament's fastest goal after three minutes; Ellen White added to her tally five minutes before half-time; and after the break, Lucy Bronze banged in a third for the Lionesses on 57 minutes. Nikita Parris had a penalty saved by Norwegian keeper Ingrid Hjelmseth in the 83rd minute, but it didn't matter and it ended 3-0 to England.

The second quarter-final pitched hosts France against holders USA. It was an extremely hot day and the atmosphere in the stadium was electric, but USA seized their chances. Megan Rapinoe scored for them in both the fifth and the 65th minutes. Towards the end it became frenetic, and Wendie Renard got a French goal in the 81st minute, but it finished 2-1 to USA.

All but one of the Italian players were amateurs and they had done exceptionally well to reach the quarter-finals, but although they matched the Dutch for most of the game and it remained 0-0 until the last 20 minutes, their opponents finally managed to get the upper hand and Sherida Spitse free kicks led to goals from first Vivianne Miedema and then Stefanie van der Gragt. Netherlands won 2-0.

Finally, in the fourth quarter-final Sweden faced off against Germany with the Germans taking an early lead through Lina Magull after 16 minutes. However, it didn't take long – six minutes to be precise – for Sofia Jakobsson to equalise for Sweden and then, three minutes after the restart, Stine Blackstenius got what proved to be the winner. This one had been quite hard to call, but it was 2-1 to Sweden.

Next it was the semi-finals and England had tough opponents in the USA. Christen Press opened for the Americans with a header on ten minutes, but Ellen White hit back with nine minutes later. Another header for USA, this time from Alex Morgan on 30 minutes, took it to 2-1 and, due to VAR disallowing another from Ellen White and USA keeper Alyssa Naeher saving a Steph Houghton penalty, that's where it stayed.

When Netherlands and Sweden met, both goalkeepers – Sari van Veenendaal for the Dutch and Hedwig Lindahl for the Swedes – very much kept their respective teams' hopes alive and it was still 0-0 at the end of 90 minutes. Nine minutes in to extra-time, though, Jackie Groenen sent the Netherlands through 1-0 when she hit a long-distance shot that Lindahl just couldn't get to.

England and Sweden lined up for the third-place play-off, but England's defenders were caught napping and Kosovare Asllani got the first goal, for Sweden, after 11 minutes, and then Sofia Jakobsson got the second, also for Sweden, after 22 minutes. England's Fran Kirby 31st-minute shot went in off the post, but, for the second time in two games, Ellen White's equaliser was ruled out by VAR. It was 2-1 and Sweden had come third in the competition overall, while USA and Netherlands would battle it out in the final.

FACT FOCUS

When France was knocked out in the 2019 quarter-finals, they joined the list of six host nations who had exited the tournament at this stage. Only USA in 1999 and 2003 progressed further – they won in 1999, although in 2003 they lost in the semi-finals to Germany, but beat Canada in the third-place play-off.

WWC FRANCE 2019 | QUARTER-FINALS AND SEMI-FINALS

England's Steph Houghton jumps in an aerial duel with USA's Alex Morgan in the 2019 semi-final.

THE HISTORY OF THE WOMEN'S WORLD CUP

Goalkeeper Sari Van Veenendaal at the ready as Netherlands defend a corner in their semi-final against Sweden.

THE HISTORY OF THE WOMEN'S WORLD CUP

▼ Christen Press of the USA and Sherida Spitse of the Netherlands battle for possession during the 2019 Final.

WWC FRANCE 2019 | FINAL

2019 FINAL

USA 2-0 NETHERLANDS

The sun was shining – in fact, it was extremely hot – and 58,000 fans were packed into the Stade de Lyon for the Women's World Cup 2019 final as underdogs Netherlands faced the top-ranked defending champions USA. Both teams had women coaches – Jill Ellis for USA, Sarina Wiegman for Netherlands – and both teams started brightly, as if to signal that they meant business.

In the first half, Sari van Veenendaal and her Netherlands goal came under a great deal of pressure from the Americans, playing their usual four-three-three formation, but the Dutch defence successfully managed to repel all-comers. Midfielder Sherida Spitse picked up a yellow card in the process, as did USA defender Abby Dahlkemper, when the Dutch counter-attacked and she fouled Dutch forward Lineth Beerensteyn. However, despite all the pressure, when they went in at half-time it was still 0-0.

When they came back out, the physical challenges from both sides continued, with USA defender Becky Sauerbrunn receiving a nasty cut to her face. The breakthrough for USA came just over quarter of an hour into the second half when Alex Morgan, who was trying to get the ball under control in the area, was kicked in the shoulder by Dutch defender Stefanie van der Gragt. At first the foul went unnoticed by French referee Stéphanie Frappart, but it was picked up by VAR and a penalty was awarded. Megan Rapinoe stepped up to take it and calmly slotted the ball past van Veenendaal – at the time it's unlikely this was on her mind, but at 34 Rapinoe was the oldest player to score in a Women's World Cup final. Having got one, USA got another eight minutes later, when Rose Lavelle's high-velocity shot hit the back of the net.

The Netherlands were losing 2-0 and the USA attacks kept coming, so defender Anouk Dekker came off and was replaced by forward Shanice van de Sanden, who forced a save from experienced USA keeper Alyssa Naeher. Morgan, Tobin Heath and Crystal Dunn for USA continued to make concerted efforts to extend that 2-0 lead further, although Spitse and Jill Roord for Netherlands also came close to cancelling it out. However, at the final whistle, USA were champions of the world and had won the Women's World Cup for a staggering fourth time.

It was one of the tightest Golden Boot contests in the history of the Women's World Cup, with three players – England's Ellen White, and USA's Megan Rapinoe and Alex Morgan – finishing on six goals apiece. Based on assists, Rapinoe took gold, Morgan silver and White bronze. Of course, had White not had two goals disallowed by VAR she would have won the Golden Boot easily. The Golden Ball also went to Rapinoe, with England's Lucy Bronze being awarded the Silver Ball and Rose Lavelle, also of USA, receiving the Bronze Ball.

At this tournament, Megan Rapinoe, distinctive with her purple hair and straight-talking attitude, became a global star and international icon. She lifted the trophy, but she also spoke out with great eloquence – about equality in sport, about the position of gay women in football and about US President Donald Trump's government.

MAGIC MOMENT

Birgit Prinz was first to feature in three finals, when she played in the 1995 (Germany were the runners-up on that occasion), 2003 and 2007 games. In 2019, USA celebrated the fact that five of their number had also played in the 2011 (when USA were the runners-up) and 2015 finals. They were Tobin Heath, Ali Krieger, Carli Lloyd, Alex Morgan and Megan Rapinoe.